Col

BELFAST

Contents

Key to map pages	2
Distance chart	2
Key to map symbols	3
Route planning map	4-5
Belfast information	6-7
Main Belfast maps	8-29
Central Belfast map	30-31
Index to place names	32
Index to street names	32-47
Tourist & travel information	48

Published by Collins
An imprint of HarperCollins Publishers
77-85 Fulham Palace Road, Hammersmith, London W6 8JB

www.harpercollins.co.uk

Copyright © HarperCollins Publishers Ltd 2009

Collins® is a registered trademark of HarperCollins Publishers Limited

Mapping generated from Collins Bartholomew digital databases

Based upon the Ordnance Survey of Northern Ireland mapping with the permission of the Controller of Her Majesty's Stationery Office. © Crown copyright. Permit number 80194

Belfast population derived from the 2001 Census.
Source: Northern Ireland Statistics and Research Agency www.nisra.gov.uk
Reproduced by permission.

Fixed speed camera information supplied by PocketGPSWorld.Com Ltd

Printed in Hong Kong

ISBN 978 0 00 725757 7   Imp 01   VI12343 / CDL

e-mail: roadcheck@harpercollins.co.uk

Key to map pages

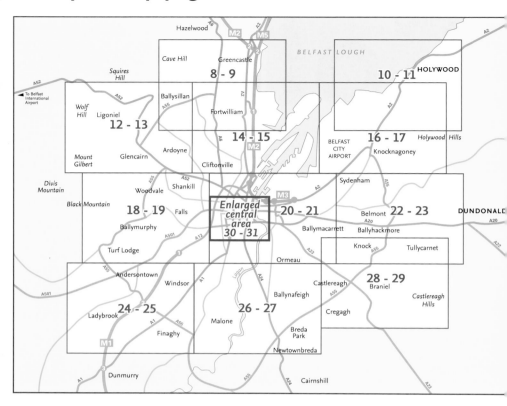

Distance chart

The distance between two selected towns will be found at the intersection of the respective rows and columns, e.
distance between Belfast and Dublin is 104 miles/166 kilometres. In general, distances are based on the shortest
routes by classified roads.

DISTANCE IN KILOMETRES

Athlone	266	130	214	182	125	144	93	125	230	261	120	208	64	208	117	187	173
	Belfast	291	422	179	166	83	304	283	434	35	322	117	267	328	205	426	331
		Castlebar	283	150	242	251	80	248	293	326	182	221	189	349	86	285	296
			Cork	400	256	323	208	147	86	459	104	426	152	206	334	118	125
141				Donegal	221	157	203	307	405	189	294	69	245	389	66	408	355
81	182				Dublin	85	218	117	307	202	197	235	123	162	216	301	157
134	264	177				Dundalk	237	197	350	118	240	155	186	245	166	344	242
114	112	94	250				Galway	155	192	339	104	270	109	272	138	162	219
78	104	151	160	138				Kilkenny	197	318	112	333	50	99	243	213	48
90	52	157	202	98	53				Killarney	469	110	438	182	274	341	32	192
58	190	50	130	127	136	148				Larne	358	115	301	363	240	462	366
78	177	155	92	192	73	123	97				Limerick	346	74	210	230	104	128
144	271	183	54	253	192	219	120	123				Londonderry	290	395	134	430	381
163	22	204	287	118	126	74	212	199	293				Roscrea	160	181	176	109
75	201	114	65	184	123	150	65	70	69	224				Rosslare	325	290	82
130	73	138	266	43	147	97	169	208	274	72	216				Sligo	285	291
40	167	118	95	153	77	116	68	31	114	188	46	181				Tralee	208
130	205	218	129	243	101	153	170	62	171	227	131	247	100				Waterford
73	128	54	209	41	135	104	86	152	213	150	144	84	113	203			
117	266	178	74	255	188	215	101	133	20	289	65	269	110	181	178		
108	207	185	78	222	98	151	137	30	120	229	80	238	68	51	182	130	

DISTANCE IN MILES

Key to map symbols 3

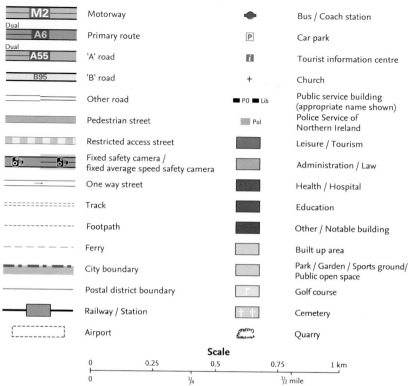

M2 Dual	Motorway
A6 Dual	Primary route
A55	'A' road
B95	'B' road
	Other road
	Pedestrian street
	Restricted access street
	Fixed safety camera / fixed average speed safety camera
	One way street
	Track
	Footpath
	Ferry
	City boundary
	Postal district boundary
	Railway / Station
	Airport

	Bus / Coach station
P	Car park
i	Tourist information centre
+	Church
PO Lib	Public service building (appropriate name shown)
Pol	Police Service of Northern Ireland
	Leisure / Tourism
	Administration / Law
	Health / Hospital
	Education
	Other / Notable building
	Built up area
	Park / Garden / Sports ground / Public open space
	Golf course
	Cemetery
	Quarry

Scale

0   0.25   0.5   0.75   1 km
0   ¼   ½ mile

1:14,900   4¼ inches (10.8 cm) to 1 mile / 6.7 cm to 1 km

Key to map symbols (pages 4-5)

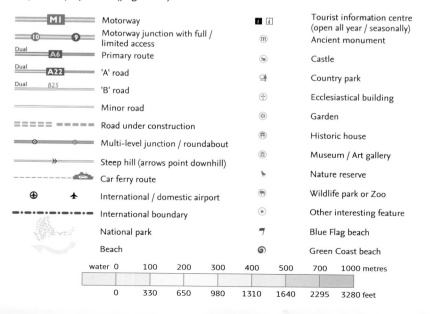

M1	Motorway
10 — **9**	Motorway junction with full / limited access
A6 Dual	Primary route
A22 Dual	'A' road
B25 Dual	'B' road
	Minor road
	Road under construction
	Multi-level junction / roundabout
»	Steep hill (arrows point downhill)
	Car ferry route
⊕ ✈	International / domestic airport
	International boundary
	National park
	Beach

i i	Tourist information centre (open all year / seasonally)
m	Ancient monument
⋒	Castle
⌂	Country park
⊕	Ecclesiastical building
✿	Garden
⌂	Historic house
🏛	Museum / Art gallery
↳	Nature reserve
🐾	Wildlife park or Zoo
✶	Other interesting feature
⌐	Blue Flag beach
◉	Green Coast beach

water 0   100   200   300   400   500   700   1000 metres
0   330   650   980   1310   1640   2295   3280 feet

4

Roe Valley
Aghadowey Finvoy Dunloy New Crom Cloughmills
ysteel Lackagh Glenhead Drumsurn Moneydig Vow
Garvagh Kilrea Glarryford Clogh
Gortnahey Bovedy Craigs
Cross Roads Craigavole Cullybackey A26 A4
Foreglen Dungiven Boviel Lislea Portglenone M2
Claudy Craigdarragh Swatragh Tamlaght O'Crilly Gracehill
Feeny Upperlands Inishrush A42 Clady A42 Ahoghill
Park Banagher Glen Culnady A54 New Ferry Straid
Maghera Gulladuff Lough Beg Grange Corner Caddy
Sawel Mt. Sperrin Mountains Moneyneany Knockcloghrim Bellaghy Moneyglass
Mount Hamilton Draperstown Tobermore Curran Castledawson Roxhill
Cranagh The Six Towns Desertmartin Toome Randalstown
Mullaghmore Magherafelt A6 M22 Mill Town
Rousky Glenhull Slieve Gallion A31 A29 Staffordstown ANTR
Greencastle Moneymore The Loup Ballyronan
Dunnamore Wellbrook Beetling Mill Springhill & Costume Museum (NT)
Creggan Lissan Oritor A505 A29 Derrychrin Belfast Internation Aldergrove
Carrickmore Cookstown Coagh Moortown Crun
Pomeroy Ballinderry Ardboe Gle
Sandholes Tullyhogue The Diamond
The Rock Lough Neagh
Sixmilecross Newmills Stewartstown Lower Ballinderry
Cappagh Carland Killeen Mountjoy
Mullaghmassa Donaghmore Coalisland Aughamullan Oxford Island Aghalee Aghag
Slievemore Castlecaulfield Ballynakilly Clonoe Maghery Discovery Cen Soldierst
Dungannon A45 Milltown Bannfoot Derrytrasna
Granville Irish World Laghy Corner Peatlands Pk Derrymacash Lurgan
A5 Moygashel A29 The Argory (NT) Ardress House (NT) M1 Craigavon A26
Ballygawley Eglish Moy Charlemont Scotch Street Waringstown Bleary
Carnteel Benburb Blackwatertown Cox's Hill Portadown
Aughnacloy Crilly Dyan Benburb Valley Loughgall Ballyleny A50
Augher Caledon Navan Fort Richhill Laurelvale A26
ogher Carrickroe Tynan Cross Cath (R.C.) Armagh Hamilton's Bawn Tandragee Gilford
Emyvale Killylea St. Patrick's Trian Millford Clare Scarva A51
Glaslough Castle Leslie Tynan Palace Stables Heritage Cen Loughbrickland A27
Tedavnet Middletown Markethill Acton Poyntz Pass
Bellanode County Mus A3 Tassagh Clady Milltown Mount Norris
Monaghan (Muineachán) Tyholland Keady Glenanne Lurganar
Smithborough Castleshane Darkley Carrigatuke Whitecross A28
Three Mile Clontibret Bessbrook A1

Route planning map 5

Carnlough
Glenarm
The Maidens or Hulin Rocks
TROON CAIRNRYAN
FLEETWOOD
A42
Black Hill 383
A2
B97
Antrim
Clegagn
Corner
own
own Corner
ghshane
437 Slemish
NA
The Sheddings
Carncastle
Ballygalley
CARNFUNNOCK
Larne
STRANRAER
Shoptown
Millbrook
Kilwaughter
A8
Glynn
Island Magee
Millbay
A36
orfields
Kells
Glenoe
A2
B90
Ballystrudder
A8
Ballycarry
Black Head
ballyeaston
Ballynure
Straid
Whitehead
BIRKENHEAD (Apr-Sept) DOUGLAS (summer only)
Burnside
Doagh
Belmont
Mew Island
Newmill
Ballyclare
A57
Eden
CARRICKFERGUS
Copeland Island
Parkgate
M2
Mossley
A2
Greenisland
CRAWFORDSBURN
Groomsport
Templepatrick
A8(M)
Helen's Bay
BANGOR
Mallusk
ZOO
Belfast Lough
FOLK & TRANSPORT MUS.
HERITAGE CEN.
Donaghadee
BELFAST CASTLE
CAVE HILL
M5
Holywood
A48
A2
NEWTOWNABBEY
Ligoniel
BELFAST CITY
REDBURN
Conlig
Millisle
A52
Craigantlet
A21
BELFAST
A55
NEWTOWNARDS
SCRABO
Hannahstown
Dundonald
A20
Ballywalter
yford
Dunmurry
Castlereagh
A22
A21
MOUNT STEWART (NT)
Ards Peninsula
B5
A501
Comber
Greyabbey
A24
Moneyreagh
A21
CASTLE ESPIE WILDFOWL & WETLANDS TRUST
LISBURN
M1
Drumbo
Carryduff
A23
Lisbane
Kircubbin
A20
Ballyhalbert
A30
Hillhall
Ballygowan
Ardmillan
Killinchy
Rubane
Portavogie
azetown
The Temple
Kilmood
Strangford Lough
Culcavy
Ravernet
Saintfield
Curragh
Kirkistown
Ringboy
Hillsborough
ROWALLANE GDN. (NT)
Darragh Cross
Raffrey
A22
Cloghy
A49
Annahilt
A21
Listooder
A7
Shrigley
Killyleagh
EXPLORIS
Kearney
Kearney Pt.
Dromore
Ballynahinch
Crossgar
CASTLE WARD (NT)
A2
Portaferry
B2
Ballykeel
Kilmore
DELAMONT
A25
Strangford
Kinallen
The Spa
Drumaness
COUNTY MUS.
Raholp
Churchtown
Waringsford
Dromara
Saul
Ballyquintin Point
Slieve Croob 535
Loughinisland
Downpatrick
CATH.
A2
Drumaroad
A24
BUTTERFLY HO. & GDNS.
Seaforde
A25
CHURCH
Ballyhornan
Katesbridge
Clough
Ballynoe
Scollogstown
Church Ballee
Moneyslane
Leitrim
Annsborough
Ballykinler
Ardglass
Ballyward
Castlewellan
A2
Killough
Ballyroney
A50
Dundrum
Minerstown
Kilcoo
Bryansford
Maghera
MURLOUGH
Newcastle
Slieve Donard
Dundrum Bay

0   2   4   6 miles
0 2 4 6 8 10 km

Belfast information

General information

Population 276,459. The capital of Northern Ireland. Sited on the River Lagan at the mouth of Belfast Lough, the city grew from a small village during the industrial revolution with industries such as linen, rope making and shipbuilding.

Tourist information

The **Belfast Welcome Centre** at 47 Donegall Place, Belfast BT1 5AD ☎ 028 9024 6609 www.gotobelfast.com provides an information and accommodation booking service.

The Northern Ireland Tourist Board website is available at www.discovernorthernireland.com

Getting around

Two bus services run in and around Belfast city. Ulsterbus transports people in and out of the city and serves all major towns and villages. Metro runs around the city, departing and terminating in the city centre. For information on Metro, Ulsterbus and Northern Ireland Railways contact **Translink** ☎ 028 9066 6630 www.translink.co.uk

The main railway station in Belfast is Central Station, East Bridge Street. For rail enquiries contact **Translink** ☎ 028 9066 6630 www.translink.co.uk

Places of interest

Queen's University   Photo © Northern Ireland Tourist Board

Buildings of architectural interest include **Belfast City Hall** which dominates Donegall Square. It is a striking classical Renaissance style building completed in 1906 and its great copper dome is a landmark throughout the city. City Hall will be closed for renovation until 2009. Nearby, the **Linen Hall Library** is Belfast's oldest library and is the leading centre for Irish and local studies in Northern Ireland. Specialising in Irish culture and politics, it also has a unique collection of early printed books from Belfast and Ulster. At Queen's University the **Queen's Visitor Centre** provides information about the university and presents a varied programme of exhibitions. Located at the heart of the campus in the Lanyon Room, the centre is named after Charles Lanyon who was the architect of the main Queen's building and many other public buildings in Ireland. Another visitor centre is the **Lagan Lookout Centre** on Donegall Quay which has a multimedia and audiovisual display explaining the history of the Lagan Weir and the industrial and cultural history of Belfast.

The extravagant **Crown Liquor Saloon** on Great Victoria Street is of historic interest. It dates from Victorian times and is one of the most famous public houses in Belfast. More recent attractions include **The Odyssey**, a multi-functional entertainment centre which includes an 10,000 seat arena, the W5 interactive discovery centre, cinema and leisure complex. Another well known city centre attraction are the colourful hand painted political murals of West Belfast. They adorn the walls and gable ends of many houses expressing the political viewpoints of the Protestant Shankill Road and the Catholic Falls Road and have become just as much a part of the tourist industry as the more traditional sites of the city. Black cab tours, with commentaries and photo stops, are available to view them.

To the north is **Belfast Castle** which overlooks the city from 122m (400ft) above sea level. Completed in 1870 by the 3rd Marquis of Donegall, this magnificent sandstone castle was refurbished over a 10 year period by Belfast City Council at a cost of more than £2m and was reopened to the public in 1988. East of the city is **Stormont Castle**, the home of the Northern Ireland Parliament. The Main Hall is open to the public and tours for groups can be arranged in advance.

Theatres, concert halls & festivals

Belfast Waterfront Hall ☎ 028 9033 4400 is Northern Ireland's premier concert and conference centre which covers a wide variety of entertainment in its flagship building. The **Grand Opera House** on Great Victoria Street ☎ 028 9024 1919 stages opera, drama, musicals, concerts and pantomime. The declining opulence of the building was restored in 1980 to transform it into a modern theatre whilst still retaining its lavish Victorian interior. **Ulster Hall**, first built in 1862 on Bedford Street ☎ 028 9032 3900, with its interior dominated by a massive English theatre organ, has been a favourite venue for concerts for over 140 years. The **King's Hall** ☎ 028 9066 5225 is another venue for concerts and gala shows. Many international and national events such as the Belfast Telegraph Ideal Home Exhibition and the Ulster Motor Show are held there. The main city centre theatre is the **Lyric Theatre** ☎ 028 9038 1081 which presents both classic and contemporary plays with an emphasis on Irish productions.

Annual events and festivals held in Belfast include the **Belfast Festival** which is held in late autumn at the campus of Queen's University and other city venues. Hosting international theatre, dance, music and comedy, it is Ireland's largest arts festival. The **Cathedral Quarter Arts Festival** is held in May to celebrate the best of the local talent as well as new international work.

Shopping

The main city centre shopping area is Donegall Place, most of which is pedestrianised. Belfast is also renowned for its selection of malls and shopping centres. **Castle Court Shopping Centre** in Royal Avenue is Northern Ireland's largest shopping centre, with over 70 shops extending over 3.4ha (8.5 acres). Opposite Castle Court is the modern **Smithfield Market** which replaced the old Victorian market destroyed by fire in 1974. The **Spires Centre and Mall** was refurbished in 1992 to become one of Belfast's most attractive buildings and is the place to shop for designer fashion and giftware.

Parks & gardens

Ormeau Park opened in 1871 and is the largest park in the centre of the city. South of the city the **National Botanic Gardens** are one of Belfast's most popular parks. The restored Palm House was built in 1840 and is one of the earliest examples of a curved glass and wrought iron glasshouse. North of the city **Belfast Zoo** is set in landscaped parkland on the slopes of Cave Hill. Over 160 species are housed there and the zoo increasingly focuses on wildlife facing extinction so has specialised collections with breeding programmes for endangered species.

National Botanic Garden

Photo © Joy Brown
Used under license from Shutterstock.com

Telephoning

If telephoning from Great Britain or Northern Ireland use the area code and telephone number. If telephoning from the Republic of Ireland replace 028 with 048 and follow with the required telephone number.

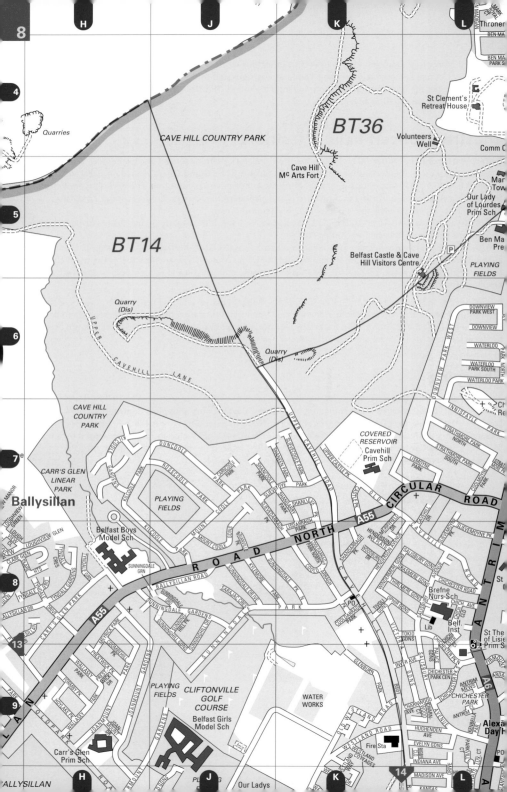

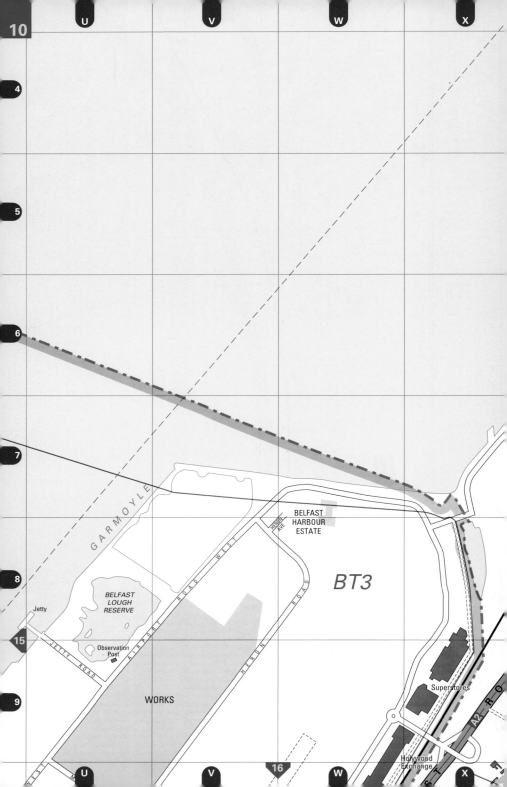

U
V
W
X

4

5

6

7

GARMOYLE

BELFAST
HARBOUR
ESTATE

BT3

8

BELFAST
LOUGH
RESERVE

Jetty

15

JETTY ROAD

Observation
Post

AIRPORT ROAD WEST

HERON ROAD

Superstores

9

WORKS

A2 R-O

Holywood
Exchange

U
V

16

W
X

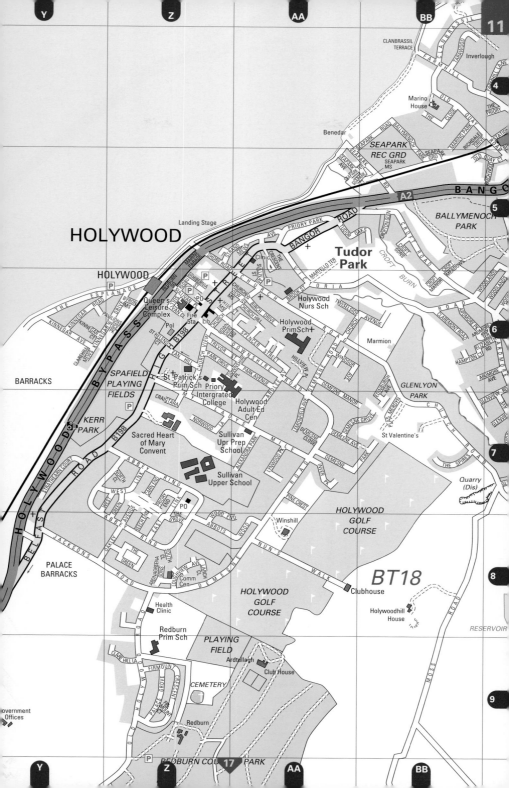

B C D E

7

TO BELFAST
INTERNATIONAL AIRPORT

A52

CRUMLIN

RUSH RD

LIGONIEL   ROAD

8

Quarry
(Dis)

Wolfhill
Manor

MILL
POND

MILL AVE

MILL
POND

WOLFHILL
GRO

WOLFHILL DR

WOLFHILL
AVENUE

MILL AVE

LEVEL ST

LEGANNEA PL

LEGANNEA ST

BOODLES
LANE

LIGONIEL

LIGONIE

MOUNTAIN

HEATHERSHILL

LIGONIEL PL

HEATHERSHILL

Wolf   Hill

MILL
POND

THORNBERRY

HORNBE

THORNBERRY ROAD

SOUTH

WOLFHILL

GLENSIDE

LIGONIEL RIVER

Glenside

9

Ligoniel

Community
Centre

MILL VALLEY PL

MILL VALLEY PK

MILL VALLEY DR

MILL VALLEY
COURT

MILL VALLEY
CRES

MILL VALLEY

Crow Glen

FORTH

MILL   RACE

WOLFHILL   ROAD

RIVER

10

NORTHRIVER   PARK

FORTH RIVER

Mount Gilbert

STANDING STONE

BT13

11

GLEN-
CAIRN

GLEN.
CAIRN

RD

Monks
Hill

GLENCAIRN

12

Divis

Mountain

BALLYGOMARTIN

WESTWA

18

B C D E

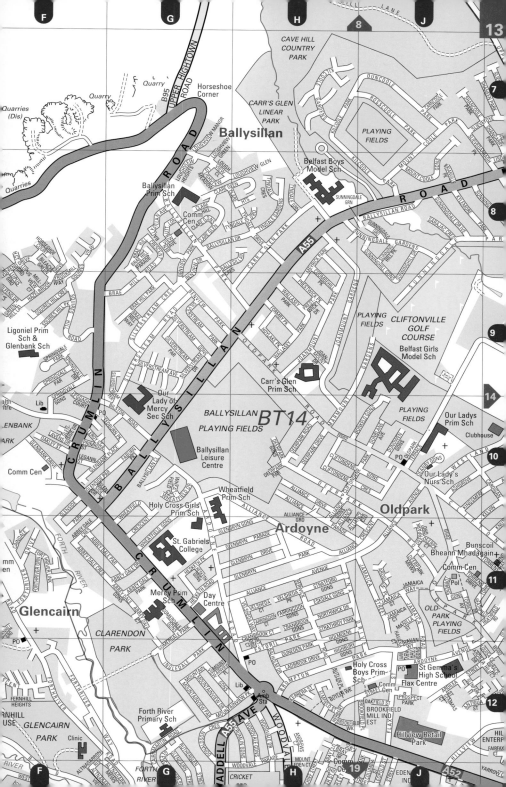

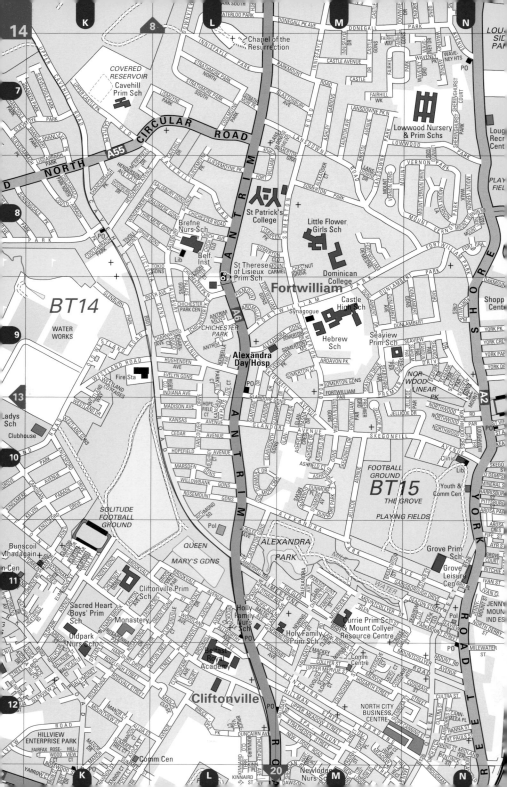

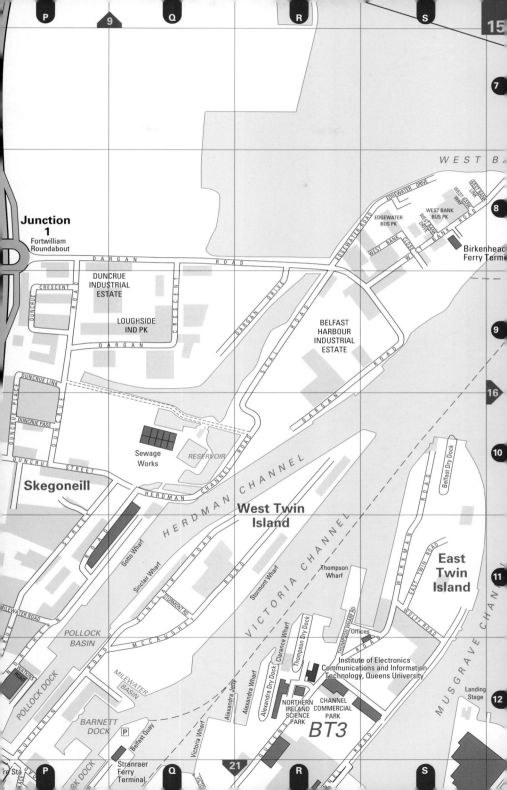

8

WEST BA

EDGEWATER DRIVE

WEST BANK LINK
WEST BANK WA
WEST BANK ROAD
WEST BANK DRIVE

WEST BANK
BUS PK

EDGEWATER
BUS PK

WEST BANK CLOSE

WEST BANK

Birkenhead
Ferry Termi

Junction 1
Fortwilliam
Roundabout

DARGAN ROAD

EDGEWATER ROAD

DUNCRUE CRESCENT

DUNCRUE
INDUSTRIAL
ESTATE

LOUGHSIDE
IND PK

CRESCENT ROAD

DARGAN DRIVE

SEAL ROAD

BELFAST
HARBOUR
INDUSTRIAL
ESTATE

DARGAN ROAD

9

DUNCRUE LINK

DUNCRUE PLACE

DUNCRUE PASS

DUNCRUE

DUNCRUE STREET

16

10

Sewage
Works

RESERVOIR

CHANNEL ROAD

Belfast Dry Dock

Skegoneill

HERDMAN HERDMAN CHANNEL

**West Twin
Island**

VICTORIA CHANNEL

**East
Twin
Island**

11

STREET

ROAD

Gotto Wharf

Sinclair Wharf

SINCLAIR

STORMONT RD

ROAD

Stormont Wharf

Thompson
Wharf

WORKMAN ROAD

EAST TWIN ROAD

WOLFF ROAD

MUSGRAVE CHAN

MILEWATER ROAD

NORTHERN

DRIVE

WATKINS ROAD

**POLLOCK
BASIN**

MCCAUGHEY

ROAD

Clarence Wharf

Thompson Dry Dock

THOMPSON WHARF RD

Offices

Institute of Electronics
Communications and Information
Technology, Queens University

Landing
Stage

12

POLLOCK DOCK

DUFFERIN ROAD

**MILEWATER
BASIN**

Alexandra Jetty

Alexandra Wharf

Alexandra Dry Dock

Victoria Wharf

Thompson Dry Dock

**NORTHERN
IRELAND
SCIENCE
PARK**

**CHANNEL
COMMERCIAL
PARK**

BT3

**BARNETT
DOCK**

P

Belfast Quay

QUEENS ROAD

ird Sta

RK DOCK

Stranraer
Ferry
Terminal

T U 10 V W

7

8

BELFAST HARBOUR ESTATE

ST BANK

WEST BANK LINK

Birkenhead Ferry Terminal

Jetty

GARMOYLE

BELFAST LOUGH RESERVE

Observation Post

JETTY ROAD

AIRPORT ROAD WEST

HERON ROAD

9

BT3

WORKS

15

10

MOSCOW ROAD

AIRPORT ROAD WEST

Superst

THE TILLYSBURN URBAN WILDLIFE RESERVE

DEPOT ROAD

11

VE CHANNEL

GEORGE BEST BELFAST CITY AIRPORT

P

BLANCHFLOWER PARK

Glendhu Nurs Sch

R—O—A—D

A55

FOOTBALL GRD

B505

TILLY

Terminal Building

12

Jetty

anding

P

AIRCRAFT PARK

Joss Cardwell Centre

HOLYWOOD

MARMONT

MARMONT DR

MARMONT CRES

Mit Ho Spec

+

T U 22 ORTS GRD V W

Bathing Pool

PASS

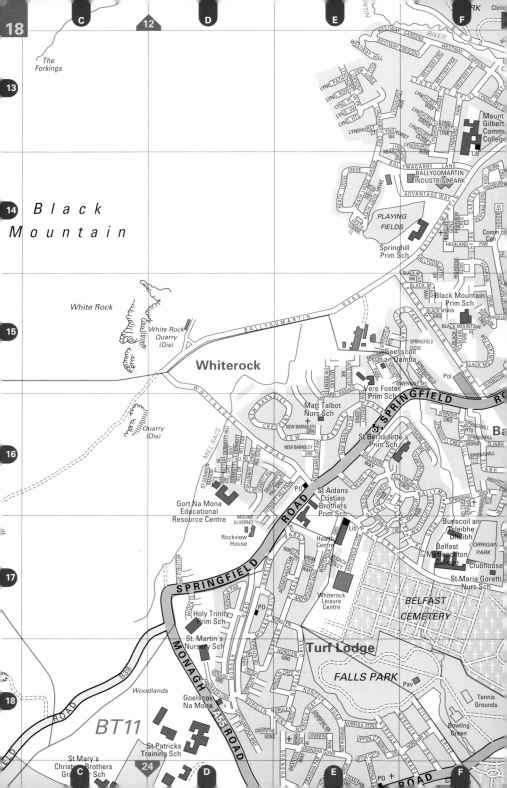

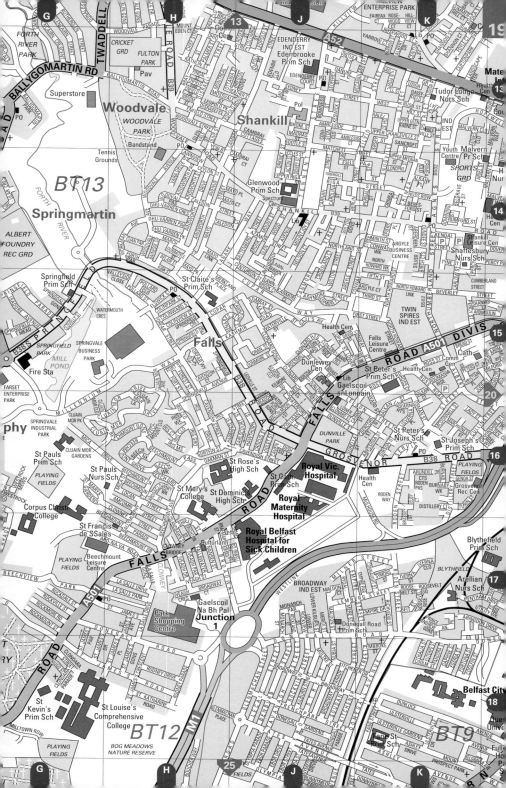

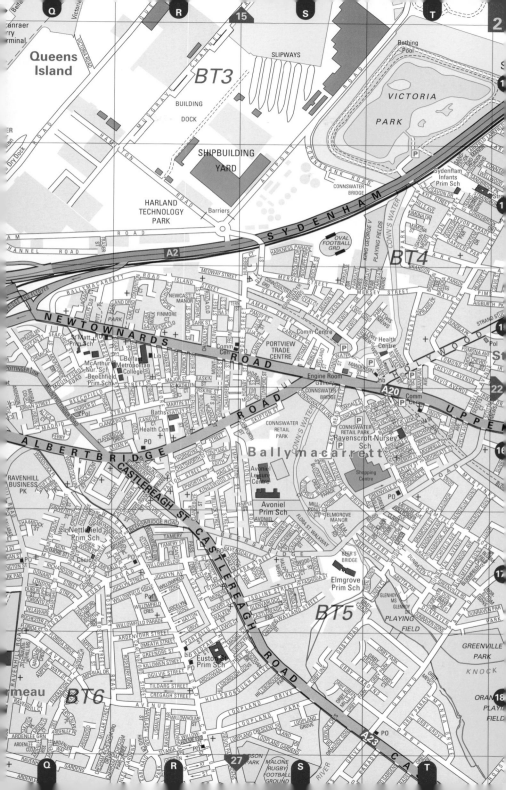

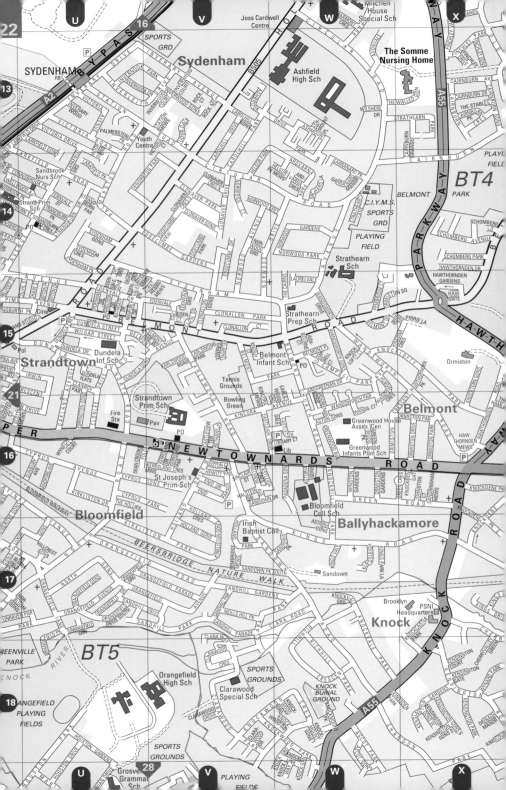

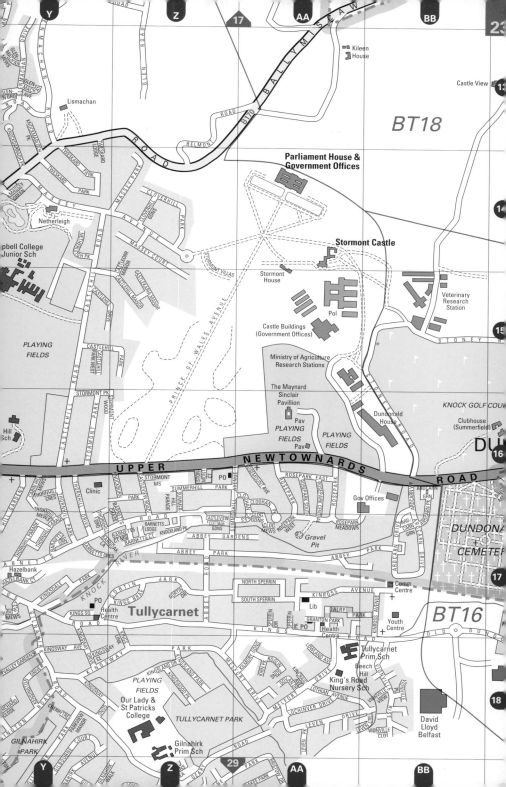

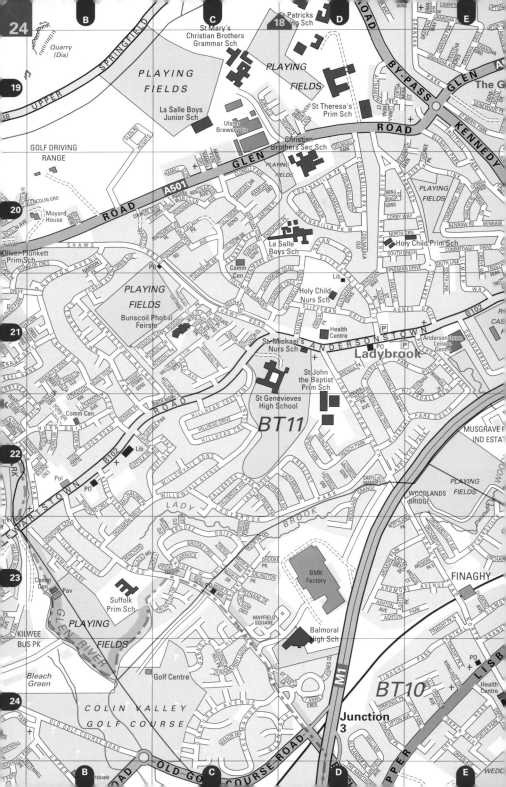

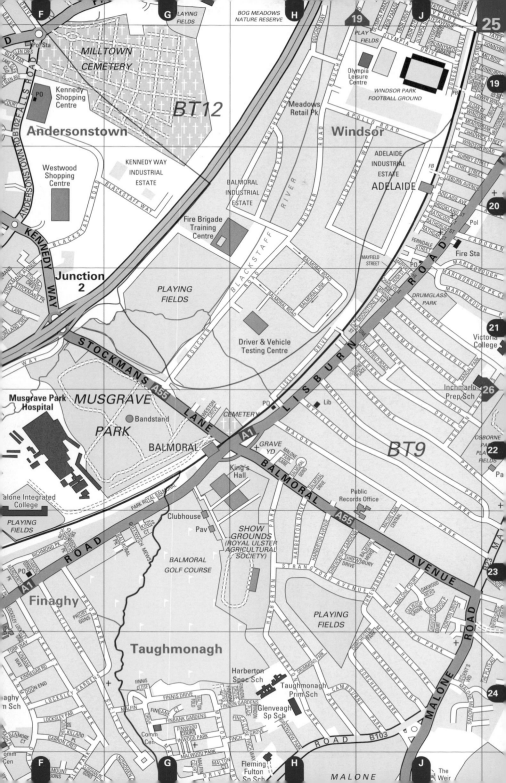

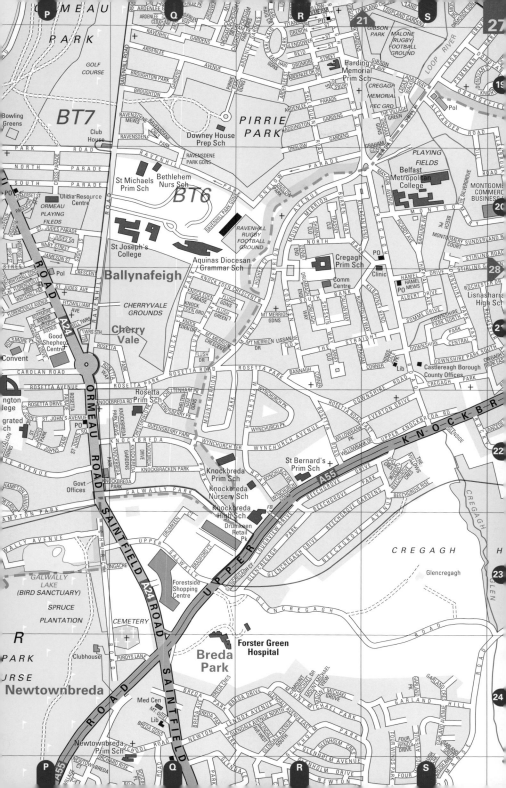

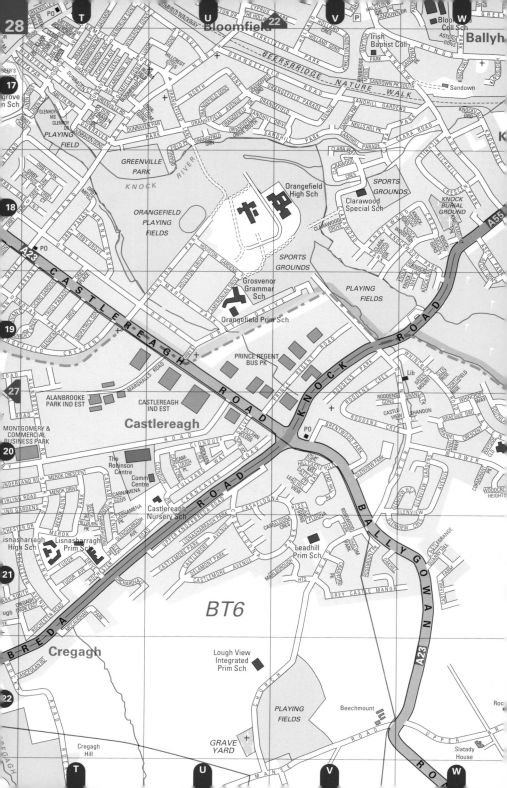

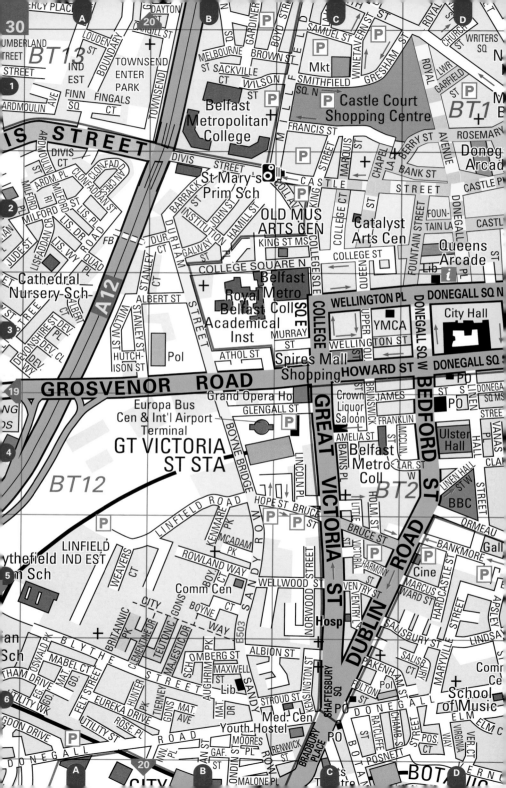

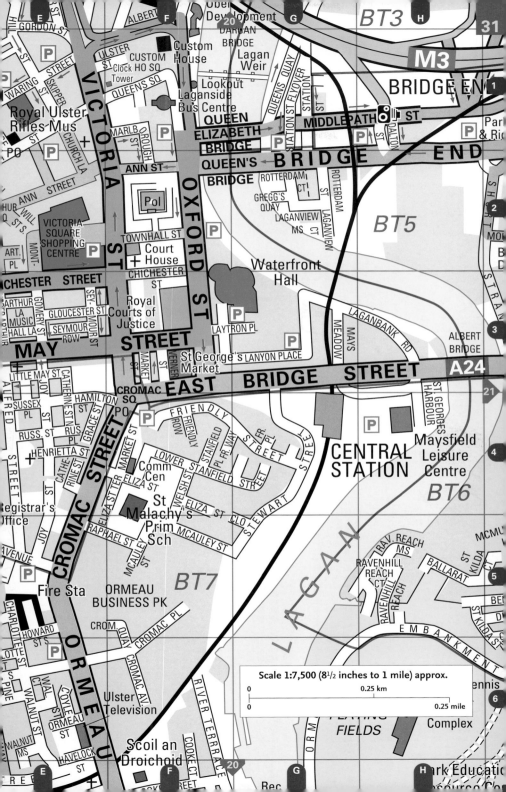

Index to place names

Andersonstown	25	F19	East Twin Island	15	S11	Queens Island	21	Q13
Ardoyne	13	H11	Falls	19	H15	Rosetta	27	Q22
Ballyhackamore	22	W17	Finaghy	25	F23	Shandon Park	29	X19
Ballymacarrett	21	S16	Fortwilliam	14	M9	Shankill	19	J13
Ballymurphy	18	F16	Gilnahirk	29	Z19	Skegoneill	15	P10
Ballynafeigh	27	P21	Glen, The	24	E19	Springmartin	19	G14
Ballysillan	13	G7	Glencairn	13	F11	Strandtown	22	U15
Belmont	22	X16	Greencastle	9	N4	Sydenham	22	V13
Bloomfield	22	U16	Holywood	11	Y5	Taughmonagh	25	G24
Braniel	28	W1	Knock	22	W17	Tudor Park	11	AA5
Breda Park	27	Q24	Knocknagoney	17	Y11	Tullycarnet	23	Z17
Castlereagh	28	T20	Ladybrook	24	D21	Turf Lodge	18	E18
Castlereagh (village)	28	U22	Ligoniel	12	E9	West Twin Island	15	R10
Cherry Vale	27	Q21	Malone	26	L22	Whiterock	18	D15
Chichester Park	14	L9	Newtownbreda	27	P24	Windsor	25	H19
Cliftonville	14	L12	Oldpark	13	J10	Woodvale	19	H13
Cregagh	28	T22	Ormeau	21	Q18	Yorkgate	20	N13
Dundonald	23	BB16	Piney Lodge	26	K23			

Index to street names

General Abbreviations

All	Alley	Cts	Courts	Lo	Lodge	Sq	Square
Arc	Arcade	Dr	Drive	Lwr	Lower	St.	Saint
Av	Avenue	E	East	Mkt	Market	St	Street
Bk	Bank	Embk	Embankment	Ms	Mews	Ter	Terrace
Bri	Bridge	Fm	Farm	Mt	Mount	Vills	Villas
Cen	Centre, Central	Gdns	Gardens	N	North	Vw	View
Ch	Church	Gra	Grange	Par	Parade	W	West
Circ	Circus	Grd	Ground	Pas	Passage	Wd	Wood
Clo	Close	Grn	Green	Pk	Park	Wf	Wharf
Cor	Corner	Gro	Grove	Pl	Place	Wk	Walk
Cotts	Cottages	Ho	House	Rd	Road		
Cres	Crescent	Hts	Heights	Ri	Rise		
Ct	Court	La	Lane	S	South		

Post Town Abbreviations

Hol.	Holywood	New.	Newtownabbey

Notes

The index contains some roads for which there is insufficient space to name on the map. The adjoining, or nearest named thoroughfare to such roads is shown in *italics*, and the reference indicates where the unnamed road is located off the named thoroughfare.

A

Abbey Ct BT5			
off Abbey Gdns	**23**	AA17	
Abbey Dale Ct BT14	**13**	G11	
Abbey Dale Cres BT14	**13**	F11	
Abbey Dale Dr BT14	**13**	G11	
Abbey Dale Gdns BT14	**13**	G11	
Abbey Dale Par BT14	**13**	F11	
Abbey Dale Pk BT14	**13**	G11	
Abbey Gdns BT5	**23**	Z17	
Abbey Pk BT5	**23**	Z17	
Abbey Pl, Hol. BT18			
off Abbey Ring	**11**	Z7	
Abbey Ring, Hol. BT18	**11**	Z7	
Abbey Rd BT5	**23**	Z17	
Abbey St W BT15			
off Hanna St	**14**	N12	
Abbots Wd, Hol. BT18	**11**	Z8	
Abercorn St BT9	**20**	L18	
Abercorn St N BT12	**19**	K16	
Abercorn Wk BT12			
off Abercorn St N	**19**	K16	
Aberdeen St BT13	**19**	K14	
Abetta Par BT5	**21**	S17	
Abingdon Dr BT12	**19**	K17	
Aboo Ct BT10	**24**	E24	
Abyssinia St BT12	**19**	K16	
Abyssinia Wk BT12			
off Abyssinia St	**19**	K16	
Academy St BT1	**20**	M14	
Acton St BT13	**19**	J14	
Adelaide Av BT9	**25**	J20	

Adelaide Chase BT9	**26**	K20	
Adelaide Pk BT9	**26**	K20	
Adelaide St BT2	**30**	D3	
Adela Pl BT14	**20**	L13	
Adela St BT14	**20**	L13	
Advantage Way BT13	**18**	F14	
Agincourt Av BT7	**26**	M19	
Agincourt St BT7	**20**	N18	
Agnes Cl BT13	**19**	K13	
Agnes St BT13	**19**	K14	
Agra St BT7	**26**	N19	
Aigburth Pk BT4	**21**	T15	
Ailesbury Cres BT7	**26**	N21	
Ailesbury Dr BT7	**26**	N21	
Ailesbury Gdns BT7	**26**	N21	
Ailesbury Rd BT7	**26**	N21	
Ainsworth Av BT13	**19**	H14	
Ainsworth Dr BT13	**19**	H14	
Ainsworth Par BT13			
off Vara Dr	**19**	H14	
Ainsworth Pass BT13	**19**	H14	
Ainsworth St BT13	**19**	H14	
Airfield Hts BT11	**24**	D19	
Airport Rd BT3	**21**	S14	
Airport Rd W BT3	**21**	S14	
Aitnamona Cres BT11	**24**	D19	
Alanbrooke Rd BT6	**28**	T19	
Albany Pl BT13	**19**	K14	
Albany Sq BT13			
off Crimea St	**19**	K14	
Albert Br BT1	**31**	H3	
Albert Br BT5	**31**	H3	
Albertbridge Rd BT5	**21**	Q16	
Albert Ct BT12	**30**	A3	

Albert Dr BT6	**27**	S21	
Albert Sq BT1	**20**	N14	
Albert St BT12	**30**	A3	
Albert Ter BT12			
off Albert St	**19**	K15	
Albertville Dr BT14	**19**	K13	
Albion La BT7			
off Bradbury Pl	**30**	C6	
Albion St BT12	**30**	B6	
Alder Cl BT5	**29**	Y19	
Alexander Ct BT15	**9**	M8	
Alexander Rd BT6	**27**	S19	
Alexandra Av BT15	**14**	M11	
Alexandra Gdns BT15	**14**	L9	
Alexandra Pk, Hol.			
Alexandra Pk Av BT15	**14**	L10	
Alexandra Pl, Hol. BT18			
off Church Vw	**11**	AA6	
Alford Pk BT5			
off Melfort Dr	**23**	AA18	
Alfred St BT2	**31**	E3	
Alliance Av BT14	**13**	H11	
Alliance Cl BT14	**13**	H11	
Alliance Cres BT14	**13**	H11	
Alliance Dr BT14	**13**	H10	
Alliance Gdns BT14	**13**	H10	
Alliance Gro BT14	**13**	H10	
Alliance Par BT14	**13**	H10	
Alliance Pk BT14	**13**	H11	
Alliance Rd BT14	**13**	H10	
Alloa St BT14	**13**	H12	
Allworthy Av BT14	**14**	L11	
Altcar Ct BT5	**21**	Q16	

Altigarron Ct BT12			
off Westrock Gdns	**19**	G16	
Altnagarron Cl BT13	**19**	G13	
Altnagarron Ms BT13	**19**	G13	
Altnagarron Ri BT13	**18**	F13	
Altnagarron Vw BT13	**18**	F13	
Alton St BT13	**20**	M14	
Ambleside Ct BT13	**19**	J13	
Ambleside St BT13	**19**	J13	
Amcomri St BT12	**19**	H16	
Amelia St BT2	**30**	C4	
Ampere St BT6	**21**	Q18	
Anderson St BT5	**21**	Q16	
Andersonstown Cres BT11	**24**	E19	
Andersonstown Dr BT11	**24**	E19	
Andersonstown Gdns BT11	**24**	E19	
Andersonstown Gro BT11	**24**	E20	
Andersonstown Par BT11			
off Andersonstown Gdns	**24**	E19	
Andersonstown Pk BT11	**24**	E19	
Andersonstown Pk S BT11	**24**	E20	
Andersonstown Pk W BT11	**24**	E19	
Andersonstown Pl BT11			
off Andersonstown Pk	**25**	F19	

Name	Page	Grid
Andersonstown Rd BT11	24	D21
Andrews Ct BT13	13	H12
Anglesea St BT13		
off Beresford St	19	K14
Annadale Av BT7	26	N22
Annadale Cres BT7	26	M21
Annadale Dr BT7	26	M21
Annadale Embk BT7	26	M21
Annadale Flats BT7	26	N20
Annadale Gdns BT7	26	N21
Annadale Grn BT7	26	N21
Annadale Gro BT7	26	N21
Annadale Ms BT7	26	N21
Annadale Sq BT7	26	N21
Annadale Ter BT7	26	M21
Annadale Village BT7	26	N21
Annalee Ct BT14		
off Avonbeg Cl	14	K12
Annesley St BT14	20	L13
Annsboro St BT13		
off Sugarfield St	19	J14
Ann St BT1	31	E2
Antigua Ct BT14		
off Glenpark St	14	K12
Antigua St BT14	13	J12
Antrim Cl BT15	14	L9
Antrim Ms BT15	14	L9
Antrim Rd BT15	8	L8
Antrim St BT13	20	L14
Apollo Rd BT12	25	H19
Appleton Pk BT11	24	D22
Apsley St BT7	30	D5
Arbour St BT14	14	K11
Ardavon Pk BT15	14	M9
Ardcarn Dr BT5	23	BB17
Ardcarn Grn BT5	23	BB16
Ardcarn Pk BT5	23	BB17
Ardcarn Way BT5	23	BB16
Ardenlee Av BT6	27	Q19
Ardenlee Cl BT6	21	Q18
Ardenlee Ct BT6	21	Q18
Ardenlee Cres BT6	21	Q18
Ardenlee Dr BT6	27	R19
Ardenlee Gdns BT6	27	R19
Ardenlee Grn BT6	21	Q18
Ardenlee Par BT6	27	R19
Ardenlee Pk BT6	21	Q18
Ardenlee Pl BT6	21	Q18
Ardenlee Ri BT6	21	Q19
Ardenlee St BT6	27	R19
Ardenlee Way BT6	21	Q18
Ardenvohr St BT6	21	R18
Ardenwood BT6	21	Q18
Ardglen Pl BT14	13	J11
Ardgowan Dr BT6	21	S18
Ardgowan St BT6	21	S18
Ardgreenan Cres BT4		
off Campbell Pk Av	22	W15
Ardgreenan Dr BT4	22	W15
Ardgreenan Gdns BT4	22	W16
Ardgreenan Mt BT4		
off Wandsworth Par	22	W16
Ardgreenan Pl BT4		
off Wandsworth Par	22	W16
Ardilaun St BT4		
off Lackagh Ct	21	Q15
Ardilea Ct BT14		
off Ardilea Dr	13	J12
Ardilea Dr BT14	13	J12
Ardilea St BT14	13	J12
Ardkeen Cres BT6	28	U20
Ardlee Av, Hol. BT18	11	AA7
Ardmillan BT15	14	L9
Ardmonagh Gdns BT11	18	E17
Ardmonagh Par BT11	18	E17
Ardmonagh Way BT11	18	E17
Ardmore Av BT7	27	P21
Ardmore Av BT10	24	D23
Ardmore Av, Hol. BT18	11	BB6
Ardmore Ct BT10	24	E23
Ardmore Dr BT10	24	D23
Ardmore Pk BT10	24	D23
Ardmore Pk, Hol. BT18	11	BB6
Ardmore Pk S BT10	24	E23
Ardmore Ter, Hol. BT18	11	BB6
Ardmoulin Av BT13	19	K15
Ardmoulin Cl BT13		
off Ardmoulin Av	30	A1
Ardmoulin Pl BT12	30	A2
Ardmoulin St BT12	30	A1
Ardmoulin Ter BT12		
off Ardmoulin St	30	A2
Ardnaclowney Dr BT12	19	H16
Ardnagreena Gdns, Hol. BT18	11	Z8
Ard-na-va Rd BT12	19	G17
Ardoyne Av BT14	13	J12
Ardoyne Ct BT14		
off Ardoyne Av	13	J12
Ardoyne Pl BT14		
off Ardoyne Av	13	J12
Ardoyne Rd BT14	13	G10
Ardoyne Sq BT14		
off Ardoyne Av	13	J11
Ardoyne Wk BT14		
off Ardoyne Av	13	J12
Ardpatrick Gdns BT6	28	T19
Ardvarna Cres BT4	22	W14
Ardvarna Pk BT4	22	W14
Argyle Ct BT13	19	K15
Argyle St BT13	19	J15
Ariel St BT13	19	K14
Arizona St BT11	24	E19
Arlington Dr BT11	24	C23
Arlington Pk BT10	24	C23
Armitage Cl BT4		
off Harkness Par	21	S14
Arney Cl BT6	27	R21
Arnon St BT13	20	M14
Arosa Cres BT15	14	N11
Arosa Par BT15	14	N10
Arosa Pk BT15	14	N11
Arran Ct BT5		
off Arran St	21	Q16
Arran St BT5	21	Q16
Artana St BT7	20	N18
Arthur La BT1	31	E3
Arthur Pl BT1	31	E2
Arthur Sq BT1	31	E2
Arthur St BT1	31	E2
Arundel Cts BT12	19	K16
Arundel Ho BT12		
off Arundel Cts	19	K16
Arundel Wk BT12		
off Roden Pas	19	K16
Ascot Gdns BT5	22	W18
Ascot Ms BT5		
off Knockmount Pk	22	W18
Ascot Pk BT5	22	W18
Ashbourne Ct BT4	22	W15
Ashbrook Cres BT4		
off Ashbrook Dr	22	W13
Ashburne Ms BT7	22	V13
Ashburne Ms BT7		
off Salisbury St	30	D5
Ashburne Pl BT7		
off Salisbury St	30	D5
Ashburn Grn BT4		
off Ashmount Pk	22	W13
Ashdale St BT5	21	S16
Ashdene Dr BT15	14	M10
Ashfield Ct BT15	14	M10
Ashfield Cres BT15	14	M10
Ashfield Dr BT15	14	M10
Ashfield Gdns BT15	14	M10
Ashford Grn BT4		
off Ashmount Pk	22	W13
Ash Grn, Hol. BT18		
off Loughview Av	11	Z8
Ashgrove Pk BT14	13	J10
Ashleigh Manor BT9	26	K19
Ashley Av BT9	19	K18
Ashley Dr BT9	19	K18
Ashley Gdns BT15	9	M7
Ashley Ms BT9	26	K19
Ashmore Pl BT13	19	J15
Ashmore St BT13	19	J15
Ashmount Gro BT4		
off Ashmount Pk	22	W13
Ashmount Pk BT4	22	W13
Ashmount Pl BT4	22	W13
Ashton Av BT10	24	D23
Ashton Pk BT10	24	D23
Aston Gdns BT4	22	W16
Astoria Gdns BT5	22	W16
Athol St BT12	30	B3
Athol St La BT12		
off Athol St	30	B3
Atlantic Av BT15	14	L11
Aughrim Pk BT12	30	B6
Ava Av BT7	26	N20
Ava Cres BT7	26	N21
Ava Dr BT7	26	N20
Ava Gdns BT7	26	N20
Ava Par BT7	26	N20
Ava Pk BT7	26	N20
Ava St BT7	26	N20
Avoca Cl BT11	18	D17
Avoca St BT14	14	K12
Avonbeg Cl BT14	14	K12
Avondale St BT5	21	T16
Avoniel Dr BT5	21	S17
Avoniel Par BT5	21	S17
Avoniel Rd BT5	21	S16
Avonorr Dr BT5	21	S17
Avonvale BT4	22	W13
Ayr St BT15	14	N11
Azamor St BT13	19	J14
B		
Back Mt St BT5	21	Q16
Baden Powell St BT13	19	K13
Bainesmore Dr BT13	19	H14
Bains Pl BT2	30	C4
Balfour Av BT7	20	P18
Balholm Dr BT14	13	H12
Balkan Ct BT12	19	K15
Balkan St BT12	19	K16
Ballaghbeg BT11		
off Bearnagh Dr	24	D20
Ballarat Ct BT6	21	Q17
Ballarat St BT6	31	H5
Ballycarry St BT14		
off Ballynure St	14	K12
Ballycastle Ct BT14	14	K12
Ballycastle St BT14		
off Ballynure St	14	K12
Ballyclare Ct BT14	14	K12
Ballyclare St BT14		
off Ballynure St	14	K12
Ballyclare Way BT14		
off Ballynure St	14	K12
Ballygomartin Dr BT13	18	F14
Ballygomartin Pk BT13	19	G13
Ballygomartin Rd BT13	18	D15
Ballygowan Rd BT5	28	V20
Ballyhanwood Rd BT5	29	AA20
Ballymacarrett Rd BT4	21	Q15
Ballymacarrett Walkway BT4		
off Dee St	21	S15
Ballymagarry La BT13	18	E14
Ballymena Ct BT14		
off Ballymoney St	14	K12
Ballymenoch Pk, Hol. BT18	11	BB4
Ballymiscaw Rd, Hol. BT18	23	AA13
Ballymoney Ct BT14		
off Ballymoney St	14	K12
Ballymoney St BT14	14	K12
Ballymurphy Cres BT12	18	E16
Ballymurphy Dr BT12	18	F16
Ballymurphy Par BT12	18	E16
Ballymurphy Rd BT12	18	F16
Ballymurphy St BT12	19	H17
Ballynure St BT14	14	K12
Ballynure Way BT14		
off Ballynure St	14	K12
Ballyroney Hill, New. BT36	9	M4
Ballysillan Av BT14	13	G8
Ballysillan Cl BT14	13	G10
Ballysillan Cres BT14	13	G8
Ballysillan Dr BT14	13	G8
Ballysillan Pk BT14	13	G8
Ballysillan Rd BT14	13	G10
Balmoral Av BT9	25	H22
Balmoral Ct BT9		
off Lisburn Rd	25	G22
Balmoral Dr BT9	25	H22
Balmoral Gdns BT9	25	H22
Balmoral Link BT12	25	H21
Balmoral Ms BT9	25	J23
Balmoral Pk (Finaghy) BT10	25	G23
Balmoral Rd BT12	25	H20
Baltic Av BT15	14	L11
Bandon Ct BT14	14	K12
Bangor Rd, Hol. BT18	11	AA5
Bankmore Sq BT7		
off Bankmore St	30	D5
Bankmore St BT7	30	D5
Bank St BT1	30	C2
Bannagh Cor BT6	27	R21
Bann Ct BT14		
off Shannon St	19	K13
Bantry St BT13		
off Kashmir Rd	19	J15
Bapaume Av BT6	27	S20
Barnetts Chase BT5	23	Z17
Barnetts Ct BT5	23	Z17
Barnetts Ct Ms BT5	23	Y17
Barnetts Cres BT5	23	Y17
Barnetts Grn BT5	23	Y17
Barnetts Lo BT5	23	Z17
Barnetts Rd BT5	23	Y17
Barnoak La BT5	23	Z17
Baroda Dr BT7	26	N19
Baroda Par BT7	26	N19
Baroda St BT7	26	N19
Barrack St BT12	30	B2
Barrington Gdns BT12		
off Abingdon Dr	19	K17
Baskin St BT5	21	R15
Bathgate Dr BT4	22	U15
Batley St BT5	21	T16
Battenberg Ct BT13		
off Battenberg St	19	H14
Battenberg St BT13	19	J14
Bawnmore Ct BT9		
off Bawnmore Rd	25	J21
Bawnmore Pk, New. BT36	9	N4
Bawnmore Pl, New. BT36		
off Newton Gdns	9	N4
Bawnmore Rd BT9	25	J21
Bawnmore Ter, New. BT36	9	N4
Bearnagh Dr BT11	24	D20
Bearnagh Glen BT11		
off Bearnagh Dr	24	D20
Bedford Sq BT2	30	D4
Bedford St BT2	30	D3
Beech End, Hol. BT18	11	Z8
Beeches, The BT7		
off Hampton Pk	26	N22
Beechfield Ct BT5		
off Beechfield St	21	R15
Beechfield St BT5	21	Q16
Beechgrove Av BT6	27	R23
Beechgrove Cres BT6	27	S22
Beechgrove Dr BT6	27	R22
Beechgrove Gdns BT6	27	R23
Beechgrove Pk BT6	27	R22
Beechgrove Ri BT6	27	S22
Beech Hts BT7	26	N22
Beechlands BT9	26	L20
Beechmount Av BT12	19	H17
Beechmount Cl BT12	19	H16
Beechmount Cres BT12	19	H16
Beechmount Dr BT12	19	H17
Beechmount Gdns BT12	19	H16
Beechmount Gro BT12	19	H16
Beechmount Link BT12	19	H16
Beechmount Par BT12	19	G16
Beechmount Pk BT12	25	F23
Beechmount Pass BT12	19	H16
Beechmount St BT12	19	H16
Beechmount Wk BT12	19	H16
Beechnut Pl BT14		
off Oldpark Rd	14	K12
Beech Pk BT6	28	T20
Beechpark St BT14		
off Oldpark Rd	14	K12
Beechview Pk BT12	19	G17

33

Name	Page	Grid
Beechwood St BT5	21	T16
Beersbridge Rd BT5	21	R17
Beit St BT12	19	K17
Belair St BT13	19	H14
Belfast Rd, Hol. BT18	16	W10
Belgrave St BT13	19	K14
Belgravia Av BT9	19	K18
Bellbashford Ct BT6		
off Woodstock Pl	21	Q16
Bell Cl BT13		
off Bootle St	19	J13
Bellfield Hts BT12	18	D17
Bell Twrs BT7	27	P21
Bell Twrs S BT7	27	P21
Belmont Av BT4	22	U15
Belmont Av W BT4	22	V15
Belmont Ch Rd BT4	22	W15
Belmont Cl BT4		
off Belmont Av	22	V15
Belmont Ct BT4		
off Sydenham Av	22	V15
Belmont Dr BT4	22	W15
Belmont Gra BT4	22	V15
Belmont Ms BT4	22	U15
Belmont Pk BT4	22	V15
Belmont Pl BT4	22	W15
Belmont Rd BT4	22	U15
Belvedere Manor BT9	26	K20
Belvedere Pk BT9	26	M22
Belvoir St BT5	21	R15
Benares St BT13	19	H15
Benbradagh Gdns BT11	24	D20
Benburb St BT12	19	J18
Bendigo St BT6	21	Q17
Ben Eden Av BT15	9	M6
Ben Eden Ct BT15		
off Ben Eden Av	9	M6
Ben Eden Grn BT15		
off Ben Eden Av	9	M6
Ben Eden Pk BT15		
off Ben Eden Av	9	M6
Ben Madigan Pk, New. BT36	8	L4
Ben Madigan Pk S, New. BT36	8	L4
Benmore Ct BT10	25	F24
Benmore Dr BT10	25	F24
Bennett Dr BT14		
off Brookvale Av	14	L11
Benraw Gdns BT11		
off Benraw Rd	24	E20
Benraw Grn BT11	24	E20
Benraw Rd BT11	24	E20
Benraw Ter BT11		
off Benraw Rd	24	E20
Bentham Dr BT12	19	K17
Bentinck St BT15	14	N12
Benview Av BT14	13	G8
Benview Dr BT14	13	G9
Benview Pk BT14	13	G9
Benwee Pk BT11	24	B22
Beresford St BT13	19	K14
Berkeley Rd BT3	20	P13
Berlin St BT13	19	J14
Berry St BT1	30	D2
Berwick Rd BT14	13	H11
Bethany St BT4	22	V16
Beverley St BT13	19	K15
Bilston Rd BT14	13	G10
Bingnian Dr BT11	24	D20
Bingnian Way BT11	24	D21
Birch Dr, Hol. BT18	11	AA6
Black Mountain Gro BT13	18	F15
Black Mountain Par BT13	18	F15
Black Mountain Pk BT13	18	F15
Black Mountain Pl BT13	18	F15
Black Mountain Wk BT13	18	F14
Black Mountain Way BT13	18	F15
Blacks Ct BT11	24	B23
Blacks Ms BT11	24	B23
Blacks Rd BT10	24	C23
Blacks Rd BT11	24	B23
Blackstaff Rd BT11	25	F20
Blackstaff Way BT11	25	G20
Blackwater Way BT12		
off Brassey St	19	K17
Blackwood St BT7	26	N20
Bladon Ct BT9	26	L23
Bladon Dr BT9	26	K22
Bladon Pk BT9	26	K22
Blakeley Ter BT12		
off Rowland Way	30	B5
Blaney St BT13		
off Crimea St	19	K13
Bleach Grn BT14	13	F8
Bleach Grn Ct BT12	18	E17
Bleach Grn Ter BT12		
off Whiterock Gro	18	E17
Blenheim Dr BT6	28	T19
Blondin St BT12	20	L18
Bloomdale St BT5	21	T16
Bloomfield Av BT5	21	T16
Bloomfield Ct BT5	21	S16
Bloomfield Cres BT5	21	S16
Bloomfield Dr BT5	21	S16
Bloomfield Gdns BT5	21	T17
Bloomfield Par BT5	21	S16
Bloomfield Pk BT5	21	T17
Bloomfield Pk W BT5	21	T17
Bloomfield Rd BT5	21	T16
Bloomfield St BT5	21	S16
Blythe St BT12	30	A6
Bombay St BT13	19	J15
Bond St BT7	31	F5
Boodles Hill BT14		
off Mountainhill Rd	12	E9
Boodles La BT14	12	E8
Bootle St BT13	19	J13
Botanic Av BT7	30	C6
Botanic Ct BT7		
off Agincourt Av	26	M19
Boucher Cres BT12	25	H19
Boucher Pl BT12	25	H20
Boucher Rd BT9	25	G21
Boucher Rd BT12	25	G21
Boucher Way BT12	25	H19
Boulevard, The BT7	26	N21
Boundary St BT13	20	A1
Boundary Wk BT13	20	L14
Boundary Way BT13	20	L14
Bowness St BT13	19	J13
Boyd St BT13	30	B1
Boyne Br BT12	30	B4
Boyne Ct BT12	30	B5
Bradbury Pl BT7	20	M18
Bradford Pl BT8		
off Church Rd	27	P23
Bradford Sq BT1		
off Steam Mill La	20	N14
Brady's La BT13		
off Boundary St	20	L14
Brae Hill Cres BT14	13	G8
Brae Hill Link BT14		
off Brae Hill Rd	13	G9
Brae Hill Par BT14	13	G8
Brae Hill Pk BT14	13	G9
Brae Hill Rd BT14	13	G9
Brae Hill Way BT14	13	G9
Braemar St BT12	19	H17
Braeside Gro BT5	28	W20
Bramcote St BT5	21	T17
Brandon Par BT4	21	T14
Brandon Ter BT4	21	T15
Brandra St BT4	21	T15
Braniel Cres BT5	28	W20
Braniel Pk BT5	28	W20
Braniel Way BT5	28	W20
Brantwood St BT15	14	M11
Brassey St BT12	19	K17
Bray Cl BT13	13	H12
Bray Ct BT13		
off Bray Cl	13	H12
Bray St BT13	19	H13
Breach Cl BT5		
off Clandeboye St	21	R16
Bread St BT12	19	K15
Breda Av BT8	27	Q24
Breda Cres BT8	27	Q24
Breda Dr BT8	27	Q24
Breda Gdns BT8	27	Q24
Breda Par BT8	27	Q24
Breda Pk BT8	27	Q24
Brenda Pk BT11	24	D21
Brenda St BT5	21	S17
Brentwood Pk BT5	28	V20
Brianville Pk BT14	8	J8
Briar Vw BT11	24	B20
Briarwood Pk BT5	29	Z19
Bridge End BT5	31	G2
Bridge End Flyover BT4	21	Q15
Bridge End Flyover BT5	21	Q15
Bridge St BT1	31	E1
Brighton St BT12	19	H17
Bright St BT5		
off Hornby St	21	R16
Bristol Av BT15	9	M7
Bristow Dr BT5	29	AA19
Bristow Pk BT9	25	H23
Britannic Dr BT12		
off Rowland Way	30	B5
Britannic Pk BT12	30	A6
Britannic Ter BT12		
off Rowland Way	30	B5
Brittons St BT12	19	G17
Brittons Dr BT12	18	F17
Brittons Par BT12	19	G17
Broadway BT12	19	H17
Broadway Ct BT12		
off Iveagh Cres	19	H17
Broadway Par BT12	19	J18
Bromfield BT9	26	K20
Bromley St BT13	19	J13
Brompton Pk BT14	13	H12
Brooke Cl BT11	24	C23
Brooke Ct BT11	24	C23
Brooke Cres BT11	24	C23
Brooke Dr BT11	24	C23
Brooke Manor BT11	24	C23
Brooke Pk BT10	24	C23
Brookfield Pl BT14	13	J12
Brookfield St BT14		
off Herbert St	13	J12
Brookfield Wk BT14	13	H12
Brookhill Av BT14	14	L12
Brookland St BT9	25	J20
Brook Meadow BT5	29	Z19
Brookmill Way BT14	13	F9
Brookmount Gdns BT13		
off Lawnbrook Av	19	J14
Brookmount St BT13	19	J14
Brook St, Hol. BT18	11	AA6
Brookvale Av BT14	14	L11
Brookvale Dr BT14	14	L11
Brookvale Par BT14	14	L11
Brookvale St BT14	14	K11
Brookville Ct BT14	14	L11
Broomhill Cl BT9	26	K22
Broomhill Ct BT9	26	K22
Broomhill Manor BT9		
off Stranmillis Rd	26	K22
Broomhill Pk BT9	26	K22
Broomhill Pk Cen BT9	26	L22
Broom St BT13	19	H13
Brougham St BT15	14	N12
Broughton Gdns BT6	27	Q19
Broughton Pk BT6	27	Q19
Brown Sq BT13	20	L14
Browns Row BT1		
off Academy St	20	N14
Brown St BT13	30	B1
Bruce St BT2	30	C4
Brucevale Ct BT14	14	L12
Brucevale Pk BT14	14	L12
Brunswick St BT2	30	C3
Bruslee Way BT15	20	M13
Brussels St BT13	19	J14
Bryansford Pl BT6	21	R17
Bryson Ct BT5		
off Mountforde Rd	21	Q15
Bryson Gdns BT5		
off Mountforde Rd	21	Q15
Bryson St BT5	21	Q15
Burghley Ms BT5	23	Y17
Burmah St BT7	26	N19
Burnaby Ct BT12		
off Distillery St	19	K16
Burnaby Pl BT12		
off Distillery St	19	K16
Burnaby Pl BT12	19	K16
Burnaby Wk BT12	19	K16
Burnaby Way BT12		
off Burnaby Pl	19	K16
Burntollet Way BT6	27	R21
Burren Way BT6	27	R20
Bute St BT15	14	N11
Butler Pl BT14	13	H12
Butler St BT14	13	J12
Butler Wk BT14	13	H12
Buttermilk Loney BT14	13	G8
Byron Pl Ms, Hol. BT18	11	Z6

C

Name	Page	Grid
Cabin Hill Ct BT4	23	Y16
Cabin Hill Gdns BT5	23	Y17
Cabin Hill Ms BT5	23	Y16
Cabin Hill Pk BT5	22	X17
Cable Cl BT4		
off Newtownards Rd	21	R15
Cadogan Pk BT9	25	J20
Cadogan St BT7	26	N19
Cairnburn Av BT4	22	X13
Cairnburn Cres BT4	22	X13
Cairnburn Dell BT4		
off Cairnburn Cres	22	X13
Cairnburn Dr BT4	22	X13
Cairnburn Gdns BT4	22	X13
Cairnburn Gra BT4	22	X14
Cairnburn Pk BT4	22	X13
Cairnburn Rd BT4	22	X14
Cairndale BT13	13	F11
Cairnmartin Rd BT13	19	G13
Cairns, The BT4	22	W15
Cairns St BT12	19	J16
Cairo St BT7	26	N19
Caledon Ct BT13	19	H14
Caledon St BT13	19	H14
California Cl BT13		
off North Boundary St	20	L14
Callan Way BT6	27	R21
Callender St BT1	30	D2
Calvin St BT5	21	R16
Camberwell Ct BT15		
off Limestone Rd	14	L11
Camberwell Ter BT15	14	L11
Cambourne Pk BT9	25	H24
Cambrai Cotts BT13	19	J13
Cambrai Ct BT13	19	H14
Cambrai St BT13	19	H13
Cambridge St BT15		
off Canning St	14	N12
Camden St BT9	20	L18
Cameronian Dr BT5	28	T19
Cameron St BT7	20	M18
Camlough Pl BT6	28	U20
Campbell Chase BT4	23	Y15
Campbell Ct BT4	22	W15
Campbell Pk Av BT4	22	W15
Canada St BT6	21	Q17
Candahar St BT7	26	N20
Canmore Cl BT13	19	J15
Canmore Ct BT13		
off Canmore St	19	J15
Canmore St BT13	19	J15
Canning Pl BT15		
off Canning St	14	N12
Canning's Ct BT13		
off Shankill Rd	19	K14
Canning St BT15	14	N12
Canterbury St BT7	20	N18
Canton Ct BT6		
off Willowfield St	21	R17
Cappagh Gdns BT6		
off South Bk	27	R21
Cappy St BT6	21	Q17
Capstone St BT9	21	H21
Cardigan Dr BT14	14	K10
Carew St BT4	21	S15
Cargill St BT13	20	L14
Carlingford St BT6	21	R18
Carlisle Circ BT14	20	L13
Carlisle Par BT15	20	M13
Carlisle Rd BT15	20	M13
off Carlisle Ter	20	M13
Carlisle Ter BT15	20	M13

34

Entry	Page	Grid
Carlisle Wk BT15		
off Queens Par	20	M13
Carlow St BT13	19	K15
Carmel St BT7	20	M18
Carnalea Pl BT15	14	N12
Carnamena Av BT6	28	T20
Carnamena Gdns BT6	28	T20
Carnamena Pk BT6	28	T21
Carnanmore Gdns BT11		
off Carnanmore Pk	24	B23
Carnanmore Pk BT11	24	B23
Carnan St BT13	19	J14
Carncaver Rd BT6	28	U20
Carncoole Pk BT14	8	J7
Carn End, Hol. BT18	11	Z7
Carney Cres BT6	28	U20
Carnforth St BT5	21	S16
Carnmore Pl BT12		
off Whiterock Rd	18	E16
Carnnamona Ct BT11	24	D19
Carolan Rd BT7	27	P21
Carolhill Dr BT4	22	V14
Carolhill Gdns BT4	22	V13
Carolhill Pk BT4	22	V14
Carolina St BT13	19	J14
Carrick Hill BT1	20	M14
Carrington St BT6	21	Q17
Carr's Glen Pk BT14	8	H8
Casaeldona Cres BT6	28	U21
Casaeldona Dr BT6		
off Casaeldona Ri	28	U20
Casaeldona Gdns BT6	28	V20
Casaeldona Pk BT6	28	U20
Casaeldona Ri BT6	28	U20
Casement Cts BT11		
off Andersonstown Rd	24	E21
Castle Arc BT1		
off Castle La	30	D2
Castle Av BT15	9	M7
Castle Chambers BT1		
off Rosemary St	30	D1
Castle Ct BT6	28	V20
Castle Ct Shop Cen BT1	30	C1
Castle Dr BT15	9	M7
Castle Gdns BT15	9	M7
Castlegrange BT5	28	W21
Castlehill Dr BT4	23	Y15
Castlehill Fm BT5	28	W21
Castlehill Manor BT4	23	Z15
Castlehill Pk BT4	23	Y15
Castlehill Pk W BT4	23	Y15
Castlehill Rd BT4	23	Y16
Castlekaria Manor BT4	23	Z15
Castle La BT1	30	D2
Castle Ms BT6	28	V20
Castlemore Av BT6	28	U21
Castlemore Pk BT6	28	U21
Castleorr Manor BT4	23	Z15
Castle Pk BT15	8	K7
Castle Pl BT1	30	D2
Castlereagh Par BT5	21	S17
Castlereagh Pl BT5	21	R17
Castlereagh Rd BT5	21	R17
Castlereagh St BT5	21	R16
Castle St BT1	30	C2
Castleton Av BT15		
off York Rd	14	N11
Castleton Gdns BT15	14	L11
Castleview Cottage Gdns BT5	23	Z17
Castleview Ct BT5	28	V20
Castleview Rd BT5	23	Z16
Castleview Ter BT4	22	V16
Castlewood Manor BT11	24	D22
Catherine Ct, New. BT36	9	N5
Catherine St BT2	31	E4
Catherine St N BT2	31	E3
Cavanmore Gdns BT11	24	C21
Cavehill Dr BT15	8	L8
Cavehill Rd BT15	8	K8
Cavendish Ct BT12	19	H15
Cavendish Sq BT12	19	J16
Cavendish St BT12	19	H16
Cawnpore St BT13	19	J15
Ceara Ct BT9	26	L20
Cedar Av BT15	14	L10
Cedar Gro, Hol. BT18	17	Y11
Centurion St BT13	19	J14
Centurion Way BT13		
off Lawnbrook Av	19	J14
Century St BT14	19	K13
Ceylon St BT13	19	H14
Chadolly St BT4	21	R15
Chadwick St BT9	25	J19
Chamberlain St BT5	21	R16
Chambers St BT7	30	C6
Channel Commercial Pk BT3	15	R12
Channing St BT5	21	S18
Chapel La BT1	30	C2
Charleville Av BT9	25	J21
Charleville St BT13	19	K13
Charlotte St BT7	31	E5
Charnwood Av BT15	14	L9
Charnwood Ct BT15	14	L9
Charters Av BT5	29	Z19
Chater St BT4		
off Tamar St	21	S15
Chatsworth St BT5	21	R16
Cheltenham Gdns BT6	27	Q22
Cheltenham Pk BT6	27	Q22
Chemical St BT5	21	Q15
Cherryhill BT9	26	L20
Cherrytree St BT5	23	Y18
Cherryvalley BT5	22	X17
Cherryvalley Gdns BT5	23	Y18
Cherryvalley Grn BT5	22	X18
Cherryvalley Pk BT5	22	X18
Cherryvalley Pk W BT5	22	X18
Cherryville St BT6	21	Q17
Chesham Cres BT6	21	R18
Chesham Dr BT6	27	Q19
Chesham Gdns BT6		
off Ardenlee Gdns	27	R19
Chesham Gro BT6	21	Q18
Chesham Par BT6	27	Q19
Chesham Pk BT6	21	Q18
Chesham Ter BT6		
off Ardenlee Gdns	27	R19
Chesterfield Pk BT6	27	Q22
Chestnut Gdns BT14	14	K11
Chestnut Gro BT5	9	M8
Cheviot Av BT4	21	T15
Cheviot St BT4	21	T15
Chichester Av BT15	8	L8
Chichester Cl BT15	8	L8
Chichester Ct BT15	8	L8
Chichester Gdns BT15		
off Antrim Rd	8	L8
Chichester Ms BT15		
off Chichester Pk Cen		
Chichester Pk Cen BT15	14	L9
Chichester Pk N BT15	8	L8
Chichester Pk S BT15	14	L9
Chichester Rd BT15	8	L8
Chichester St BT1	31	E3
Chief St BT13	19	H13
Chlorine Gdns BT9	26	L19
Chobham St BT5	21	T16
Christian Pl BT12	19	K15
Church Av, Hol. BT18	11	AA6
Church Grn, Hol. BT18		
off Spencer St	11	AA6
Church Hill, Hol. BT18	11	AA6
Churchill St BT15	20	M13
Churchland Cl, Hol. BT18	17	X11
Church La BT1	31	E1
Church Rd BT6	28	U22
Church Rd BT8	27	P23
Church Rd, Hol. BT18	11	AA6
Church St BT1	30	D1
Church Vw, Hol. BT18	11	Z6
Churchview Ct BT14		
off Glenview St	14	K12
Church Vw Ms, Hol. BT18	11	AA6
Church Wynd BT5	29	Z19
Cicero Gdns BT6	28	T19
Circular Rd BT4	22	V14
City Way BT12	30	A5
Clanbrassil Rd, Hol. BT18	11	BB4
Clanbrassil Ter, Hol. BT18	11	BB4
Clanchattan St BT15	14	M11
Clandeboye Dr BT5	21	Q16
Clandeboye Gdns BT5	21	Q16
Clandeboye St BT5	21	S17
Clanmorris St BT15	14	N12
Clanroy Par BT4	22	U15
Clara Av BT5	21	T17
Clara Cres Lwr BT5	21	T17
Clara Cres Upr BT5	21	T17
Clara Pk BT5	22	V18
Clara Rd BT5	22	V17
Clara St BT5	21	R17
Clara Way BT5	22	V17
Clarawood Cres BT5	22	V18
Clarawood Dr BT5	22	V18
Clarawood Gro BT5	22	V18
Clarawood Pk BT5	22	V18
Clarawood Wk BT5		
off Clara Way	22	V18
Clare Gdns BT14	13	G8
Clare Glen BT14	13	G8
Clare Hts BT14	13	G8
Clare Hill BT14	13	G8
Clarehill La, Hol. BT18	17	Z9
Clarehill Ms, Hol. BT18	11	Y6
Claremont Ct BT9	20	L18
Claremont Ms BT9	20	L18
Claremont Rd, Hol. BT18	11	BB6
Claremont St BT9	20	L18
Clarence Pl Ms BT1		
off Upper Arthur St	31	E3
Clarence St BT2	30	D4
Clarence St W BT2	30	D4
Clarendon Av BT5	21	T17
Clarendon Dock BT1		
off Corporation St	20	N14
Clarendon Rd BT1	20	N14
Clarkes La BT1		
off Curtis St	20	M14
Cleaver Av BT9	26	K21
Cleaver Ct BT9	26	K21
Cleaver Gdns BT9	26	L21
Cleaver Pk BT9	26	K21
Clementine Dr BT12	30	A6
Clementine Gdns BT12		
off Rowland Way	30	B5
Clementine Pk BT12		
off Clementine Dr	30	A5
Clements St BT13		
off Malvern St	20	L14
Clermont La BT6		
off Woodstock Link	21	Q16
Clifton Cres BT14	14	K12
Cliftondene Cres BT14	13	H10
Cliftondene Gdns BT14	13	H10
Cliftondene Pk BT14	13	H10
Clifton Dr BT14	14	K12
Clifton Ho Ms BT15	20	M14
Cliftonpark Av BT14	19	K13
Cliftonpark Ct BT14	14	L12
Clifton St BT13	14	M14
Cliftonville Av BT14	14	L12
Cliftonville Ct BT14	14	L11
Cliftonville Dr BT14	14	K11
Cliftonville Par BT14	14	L11
Cliftonville Rd BT14	13	J10
Cliftonville St BT14	14	K11
Cloghan Cres BT5	23	AA16
Cloghan Gdns BT5	23	AA16
Cloghan Ms BT5	23	AA17
Cloghan Pk BT5	23	AA16
Clois Cluana Pk BT11	24	C21
Cloisters, The BT7	20	N18
Clonallon Ct BT4	22	V15
Clonallon Gdns BT4	22	V15
Clonallon Pk BT4	22	V15
Clonallon Sq BT4	22	V15
Clonard St BT13		
off Clonard Hts	19	J15
Clonard Cres BT13	19	J15
Clonard Gdns BT13	19	J15
Clonard Hts BT13	19	J15
Clonard Pl BT13	19	J15
Clonard Ri BT13	19	J15
Clonard St BT13	19	J15
Clonaver Cres N BT4	22	V14
Clonaver Cres S BT4	22	V14
Clonaver Dr BT4	22	V14
Clonaver Gdns BT4	22	V14
Clonaver Pk BT4	22	V14
Clondara Par BT12	19	G18
Clondara St BT12	19	G18
Clonduff Dr BT6	28	U20
Clonelly Av BT11	24	C20
Clonfaddan Cres BT12	30	A2
Clonfaddan St BT12	30	A2
Clonlee Dr BT4	22	U16
Cloreen Pk BT9	26	L19
Close, The, Hol. BT18	11	BB4
Closnamona Ct BT11		
off Aitnamona Cres	24	E19
Clovelly St BT12	19	G15
Cloverhill Gdns BT4	23	Z14
Cloverhill Pk BT4	23	Z14
Clowney St BT12	19	H16
Cluain Mor Av BT12	19	H15
Cluain Mor Cl BT12	19	G16
Cluain Mor Dr BT12	19	G16
Cluain Mor Gdns BT12	19	H16
Cluain Mor La BT12	19	H16
Cluain Mor Pk BT12	19	G16
Cluan Pl BT5	21	Q16
Clyde Ct BT5	21	Q16
Coars La BT1		
off Curtis St	20	N14
Coburg St BT6	21	Q17
Colchester Pk BT12		
off Abingdon Dr	19	K17
Colenso Ct BT9	26	M19
Colenso Par BT9	26	M19
Coles All BT1		
off Church La	31	E2
Colinpark St BT12	19	H15
Colinton Gdns, New. BT36	9	M4
Colinview St BT12	19	H15
Colinward St BT12	19	H15
College Av BT12	30	C2
College Ct BT1	30	C2
College Dr BT7	26	N21
College Gdns BT9	20	L18
College Grn BT7	20	M18
College Grn Ms BT7	20	M18
College Hts BT7	26	N21
College Pk BT7	20	M18
College Pk Av BT7	26	M19
College Pk E BT7	26	M19
College Pl N BT1		
off College Sq N	30	B2
College Sq E BT1	30	C2
College Sq N BT1	30	B2
College St BT1	30	C2
College St Ms BT1		
off College St	30	C2
Colligan St BT13	19	J16
Collin Gdns BT11		
off South Grn	24	D20
Collingwood Av BT7	26	N19
Collingwood Rd BT7	26	N19
Collyer St BT15	14	M12
Columbia St BT13		
off Ohio St	19	J13
Colvil St BT4	22	U15
Comber Ct BT5		
off Mountforde Rd	21	Q15
Comber Gdns BT5		
off Mountforde Rd	21	Q15
Combermere St BT12		
off Stroud St	30	C6
Commedagh Dr BT11	24	E20
Commercial Ct BT1		
off Hill St	31	E1
Conduit St BT7		
off Donegall Pass	30	D6
Coniston Cl BT13	19	J13
Connaught St BT12	19	K17
Conneywarren La BT14		
off Wolfend Dr	13	F8
Connsbank Rd BT3	21	S14
Connsbrook Av BT4	21	T15
Connsbrook Dr BT4	21	T14

Name	No.	Grid
Connsbrook Pk BT4	21	T14
Connswater Gro BT4	21	S15
Connswater Link BT5	21	S16
Connswater Ms BT4	21	S15
Connswater Shop Cen BT5		
off Bloomfield Av	21	S16
Connswater St BT4	21	S15
Conor Cl BT11	24	C21
Conor Ri BT11	24	C21
Constance St BT5	21	R16
Convention Ct BT4	21	R15
Convention Wk BT4		
off Newtownards Rd	21	R15
Conway Ct BT13		
off Conway St	19	J14
Conway Link BT13	19	J15
Conway Sq BT13		
off Conway Link	19	K15
Conway St BT13	19	J15
Conway Wk BT13	19	K14
Cooke Ct BT7	31	F6
Cooke Ms BT7	20	N18
Cooke Pl BT7		
off Cooke Ms	20	N18
Cooke St BT7	20	N18
Cooldarragh Pk BT14	8	K8
Cooldarragh Pk N BT14	8	K8
Coolfin St BT12	19	K18
Coolmore St BT12	19	K18
Coolmoyne Pk BT15	8	L7
Coolnasilla Av BT11	24	D19
Coolnasilla Cl BT11	24	D19
Coolnasilla Dr BT11	24	D19
Coolnasilla Gdns BT11	24	D19
Coolnasilla Pk BT11	24	D19
Coolnasilla Pk E BT11	24	D20
Coolnasilla Pk S BT11	24	D20
Coolnasilla Pk W BT11	24	D20
Coombehill Pk BT14	8	H8
Cooneen Way BT6	27	R20
Corby Way BT11	24	D20
Cormorant Pk BT5	28	W20
Corn Mkt BT1	31	E2
Coronation Ct BT15		
off Little York St	20	N14
Corporation Sq BT1	20	N14
Corporation St BT1	20	N14
Corrib Av BT11	24	B21
Corry Link BT3	20	P13
Corry Pl BT3	20	P13
Corry Rd BT3	20	P13
Cosgrave Ct BT15		
off Mervue St	14	M12
Cosgrave Hts BT15	14	M12
Cosgrave St BT15	14	N12
Courtrai St BT13		
off Mill St W	19	J13
Court St BT13	20	L13
Coyle's Pl BT7		
off Coyle St	31	E6
Coyle St BT7	31	E6
Craigmore Way BT7		
off Apsley St	30	D5
Craigs Ter BT13		
off Dundee St	19	K14
Craigtara, Hol. BT18	11	Z7
Cranbrook St BT14	13	H11
Cranbrook Gdns BT14	13	H11
Cranburn Pl BT14		
off Lincoln Av	20	L13
Cranburn St BT14	20	L13
Cranmore Av BT9	25	J21
Cranmore Gdns BT9	25	J21
Cranmore Pk BT9	25	J21
Cranton Ct BT6	21	R17
Craven St BT13		
off Rumford St	19	K14
Crawford St BT6	28	V21
Creeslough Gdns BT11	24	B21
Creeve Wk BT11	14	E20
Creevy Av BT5	29	X20
Creevy Way BT5	29	X19
Cregagh Ct BT6		
off Cregagh Rd	27	S19
Cregagh Pk BT6	27	S21
Cregagh Pk E BT6	27	S21
Cregagh Rd BT6	21	R18
Cregagh St BT6	21	R18
Crescent, The BT7	26	N22
Crescent, The, Hol.		
BT18	11	AA5
Crescent Gdns BT7	20	M18
Crescent La BT7		
off Lower Cres	20	M18
Cricklewood Cres BT9	26	M22
Cricklewood Pk BT9	26	M22
Crimea Cl BT13	19	K14
Crimea Ct BT13	19	K14
Crimea St BT13	19	K14
Croaghan Gdns BT11		
off South Grn	24	E20
Crocus St BT12	19	J16
Croft Gdns, Hol. BT18	11	BB5
Crofthouse Ct BT5		
off Kilmory Gdns	23	AA18
Croft Manor, Hol. BT18	11	BB6
Croft Meadows, Hol.		
BT18	11	BB5
Crofton Glen, Hol. BT18	11	BB5
Croft Rd, Hol. BT18	11	BB5
Cromac Av BT7	31	E5
Cromac Pl BT7	31	F6
Cromac Quay BT7	31	F6
Cromac Sq BT2	31	F4
Cromac St BT2	31	E5
Cromwell Rd BT7	20	M18
Crosby St BT13		
off Percy Pl	20	L14
Crosscollyer St BT15	14	M12
Crossland Ct BT13	19	J15
Crossland St BT13		
off Canmore St	19	J14
Cross Par BT7	27	P20
Crown Entry BT1		
off High St	31	E2
Crumlin Gdns BT13	13	H12
Crumlin Rd BT14	12	E7
Crystal St BT5	21	T16
Cuan Par BT13	19	H14
Cuba Wk BT4	21	R15
Cullingtree Rd BT12	19	K16
Culmore Gdns BT11	24	B20
Cultra St BT15	14	N12
Cumberland St BT13	19	K14
Cumberland Wk BT13		
off Percy St	19	K14
Cupar St BT13	19	H15
Cupar St Lwr BT13	19	J15
Cupar Way BT13	19	J15
Curtis St BT1	20	M14
Curzon St BT7	26	N19
Cussick St BT9	26	K19
Custom Ho Sq BT1	31	F1
Cutters La BT9	26	M22
Cyprus Av BT5	22	U16
Cyprus Gdns BT5	22	U16
Cyprus Pk BT5	22	U16

D

Name	No.	Grid
Dairy St BT12		
off Shiels St	19	H17
Daisyfield St BT13	19	K13
Daisyhill Ct BT12		
off Westrock Gdns	19	G16
Dalebrook Av BT11	24	C22
Dalebrook Pk BT11	24	C22
Dalry Pk BT5	23	AA17
Dalton St BT5	31	H1
Damascus St BT7	20	N18
Dandy St, New. BT36	9	N4
Danesfort BT9	26	K21
Danesfort Pk Cl BT9	26	L22
Danesfort Pk Dr BT9	26	L22
Danesfort Pk Mt BT9	26	L22
Danesfort Pk Pl BT9	26	L22
Danesfort Pk S BT9	26	L22
Danesfort Pk Wd BT9	26	L22
Danns Row BT6		
off Ravenhill Rd	21	Q16
Danube St BT13	19	J13
Daphne St BT12	19	K18
Dargan Br BT1	31	G1
Dargan Br BT3	31	G1
Dargan Cres BT3	15	P9

Name	No.	Grid
Dargan Dr BT3	15	R9
Dargan Rd BT3	9	P8
Dart Hill BT11	24	E21
David St BT13	19	J15
Dawson St BT13	20	M13
Dayton St BT13	20	L14
Deacon St BT15	14	N11
Deanby Gdns BT14	13	J10
Dean Crooks Fold BT5	22	U16
Deerpark Ct BT14	13	J11
Deerpark Dr BT14	13	H10
Deerpark Gdns BT14	13	H10
Deerpark Gro BT14	13	J11
Deerpark Ms BT14	13	J11
Deerpark Par BT14	13	H10
Deerpark Rd BT14	13	H10
Dee St BT4	21	S15
Dehra Gro BT4	22	U15
Delamont Pk BT6	28	U21
Delaware St BT6	21	Q17
Delhi Par BT7	26	N19
Delhi St BT7	26	N19
Demesne Av, Hol.		
BT18	11	AA7
Demesne Cl, Hol. BT18	11	AA7
Demesne Gro, Hol.		
BT18	11	AA7
Demesne Manor, Hol.		
BT18	11	AA6
Demesne Pk, Hol. BT18	11	AA7
Demesne Rd, Hol.		
BT18	11	Z8
Denewood Dr BT11	24	E19
Denewood Pk BT11	24	E19
Denmark St BT13	20	L14
Dennet End BT6	27	R20
Denorrton Pk BT4	22	U14
Depot Rd BT3	16	W11
Deramore Av BT7	26	N21
Deramore Ct BT9		
off Deramore Pk S	26	L23
Deramore Dr BT9	26	K23
Deramore Gdns BT7	26	N21
Deramore Pk BT9	26	K23
Deramore Pk S BT9	26	K23
Deramore St BT7	27	P20
Derby Ter BT12		
off Divis St	19	K15
Derlett St BT7	26	N20
Dermott Hill Dr BT12	18	D16
Dermott Hill Gdns		
BT12	18	D16
Dermott Hill Grn BT12	18	D16
Dermott Hill Gro BT12	18	D16
Dermott Hill Par BT12	18	D16
Dermott Hill Pk BT12	18	D16
Dermott Hill Rd BT12	18	D16
Dermott Hill Way BT12	18	D16
Derrin Pas BT11	24	E20
Derryvolgie Av BT9	26	K20
Derryvolgie Ms BT9	26	K20
Derwent St BT4	21	R15
Devenish Ct BT13		
off Cupar St Lwr	19	J15
Devon Dr BT4	21	T14
Devon Par BT4	21	T14
Devonshire Cl BT12	30	A3
Devonshire Pl BT12	30	A3
Devonshire St BT12	30	A3
Devonshire Way BT12	30	A3
Dewey St BT13	19	J14
Dhu-Varren Cres BT13	19	H14
Dhu-Varren Par BT13	19	H14
Dhu-Varren Pk BT13	19	H14
Diamond Av BT10	24	E23
Diamond Gdns BT10	24	E23
Diamond Gro BT10	24	E23
Diamond St BT13		
off Dover Pl	20	L14
Dill Rd BT6	27	S20
Disraeli Cl BT13	19	H13
Disraeli Ct BT13	19	H13
Disraeli St BT13	19	H13
Disraeli Wk BT13	19	H13
off Disraeli St	13	H12
Distillery Ct BT12		
off Distillery St	19	K16
Distillery St BT12	19	K16

Name	No.	Grid
Distillery Way BT12		
off Distillery St	19	K17
Divis Ct BT12	30	A2
Divis Dr BT11	18	F18
Divismore Cres BT12	18	E16
Divismore Pk BT12	18	F16
Divismore Way BT12	18	E16
Divis St BT12	19	K15
Dock La BT15		
off Dock St	20	N13
Dock St BT15	20	N13
Dock St Ms BT15		
off Dock St	20	N13
Donaldson Cres BT13	13	G12
Donard St BT6	21	Q17
Donegall Arc BT1	30	D2
Donegall Av BT12	25	J19
Donegall Gdns BT12	19	J18
Donegall La BT1	20	M14
Donegall Par BT12	19	J18
Donegall Pk BT10	25	F23
Donegall Pk Av BT15	8	L6
Donegall Pass BT7	30	C6
Donegall Pl BT1	30	D2
Donegall Quay BT1	20	N14
Donegall Rd BT12	19	G17
Donegall Sq E BT1	30	D3
Donegall Sq Ms BT2	30	D3
Donegall Sq N BT1	30	D3
Donegall Sq S BT1	30	D3
Donegall Sq W BT1	30	D3
Donegall St BT1	20	M14
Donegall St Pl BT1		
off Donegall St	30	D1
Donegore Gdns BT11	24	B23
Donnybrook St BT9	26	K19
Donore Ct BT15		
off New Lo Rd	14	M12
Donore Pl BT15		
off Stratheden St	14	M12
Donovan Ct BT6	27	S19
Donovan Par BT6	27	S19
Doon Cotts BT11	24	B22
Doon End BT10	25	F24
Doon Rd BT11	24	B22
Dorchester Pk BT9	25	J24
Douglas Ct BT4		
off Dundela Av	22	U15
Dover Ct BT13		
off Dover St	20	L14
Dover Pl BT13	20	L14
Dover St BT13	20	L14
Dover Wk BT13		
off Dover St	20	L14
Downfine Gdns BT11	18	D18
Downfine Wk BT11	18	E18
Downing St BT13	19	K14
Downpatrick St BT4	21	S15
Downshire Ms, Hol.		
BT18	11	Z6
Downshire Par BT6	27	S20
off Hamel Dr	27	S20
Downshire Pk Cen BT6	27	S21
Downshire Pk E BT6	27	S20
Downshire Pk N BT6	27	S21
Downshire Pk S BT6	27	S21
Downshire Pl BT2		
off Great Victoria St	30	C5
Downshire Pl, Hol.		
BT18	11	Z6
Downshire Rd BT6	27	R22
Downshire Rd, Hol.		
BT18	11	Z6
Downview Av BT15	9	M6
Downview Cres BT15	9	M6
Downview Dr BT15	9	M6
Downview Gdns BT15	9	N6
Downview Lo BT15	9	M5
Downview Manor BT15	9	N6
Downview Ms BT15	9	N6
Downview Pk BT15	8	L6
Downview Pk W BT15	8	L7
Drenia BT11	24	C23
Drinagh Manor BT5	23	X18
Drive, The BT9	26	L22
Dromara St BT7	26	N19
Dromore St BT6	21	R19
Drumkeen Ct BT8	27	Q23

Street	Map	Grid
Drumkeen Manor BT8		
off Saintfield Rd	27	Q23
Drummond Pk BT9	25	H24
Drumragh End BT6	27	R21
Dublin Rd BT2	30	C6
Dublin St BT6	21	Q17
Dudley St BT7	20	N18
Dufferin Rd BT3	15	P12
Duffield Pk BT13	18	F13
Duke St BT5		
off Susan St	21	Q15
Dunbar Link BT12	20	N14
Dunbar St BT1	20	N14
Dunblane Av BT14	13	J10
Dunboyne Pk BT13	18	F15
Duncairn Av BT14	14	L12
Duncairn Gdns BT15	14	M12
Duncairn Par BT15	20	M13
Duncoole Pk BT14	8	J7
Duncrue Cres BT3	15	P9
Duncrue Link BT3	15	P9
Duncrue Pass BT3	15	P10
Duncrue Pl BT3	15	P10
Duncrue Rd BT3	15	P10
Duncrue St BT3	15	P10
Dundee St BT13	19	K14
Dundela Av BT4	22	U15
Dundela Cl BT4		
off Wilgar St	22	U15
Dundela Ct BT4		
off Dundela St	22	U15
Dundela Cres BT4	22	U15
Dundela Dr BT4	22	U15
Dundela Flats BT4	22	U15
Dundela Gdns BT4	22	U15
Dundela Pk BT4	21	T15
Dundela St BT4	22	U15
Dundela Vw BT4		
off Dundela Av	22	U15
Duneden Pk BT14	13	H12
Dunkeld Gdns BT14	13	J10
Dunlambert Av BT15	14	M9
Dunlambert Dr BT15	14	M9
Dunlambert Gdns BT15	14	N9
Dunlambert Pk BT15	14	M9
Dunlewey St BT13	19	J15
Dunlewey Wk BT13		
off Dunlewey St	19	J16
Dunluce Av BT9	19	K18
Dunmisk Pk BT11	24	E20
Dunmisk Ter BT11		
off Commedagh Dr	24	E20
Dunmisk Wk BT11	24	E20
Dunmore Av BT15	14	M10
Dunmore Ct BT15	14	M10
Dunmore Cres BT15	14	L10
Dunmore Dr BT15	14	L10
Dunmore Ms BT15	14	M10
Dunmore Pk BT15	14	M10
Dunmore Pl BT15	14	M10
Dunmore St BT13	19	J15
Dunmoyle St BT13	19	H14
Dunmurry Lo BT10	24	C24
Dunowen Gdns BT14	13	J10
Dunraven Av BT5	21	T17
Dunraven Ct BT5	21	T17
Dunraven Cres BT5	21	T17
Dunraven Dr BT5	21	T17
Dunraven Gdns BT5	21	T17
Dunraven Par BT5	21	T17
Dunraven Pk BT5	21	T17
Dunraven St BT13		
off Rumford St	19	K14
Dunvegan St BT6	21	Q17
Dunville St BT12	19	J16
Durham Ct BT12	30	A2
Durham St BT12	30	B2

E

Street	Map	Grid
Ean Hill, Hol. BT18	11	Z6
Earl Cl BT15	20	M13
Earl Haig Cres BT6	21	R18
Earl Haig Gdns BT6	21	R18
Earl Haig Pk BT6	27	R19
Earls Ct, The BT4		
off Bethany St	22	V16
Earlscourt St BT12	19	J16
Earlswood Ct BT4		
off Kincora Av	22	W16
Earlswood Gro BT4	22	W15
Earlswood Pk BT4	22	V15
Earlswood Rd BT4	22	V15
East Bread St BT5	21	S16
East Br St BT1	31	F3
Eastleigh Cres BT5	22	V16
Eastleigh Dale BT4	22	W16
Eastleigh Dr BT4	22	V16
East Link, Hol. BT18	11	Z8
Easton Av BT14	14	K11
Easton Cres BT14	14	K11
East Twin Rd BT3	15	S11
Eblana St BT7	20	M18
Ebor Dr BT12	25	J19
Ebor Par BT12	25	J19
Ebor St BT12	25	J19
Ebrington Gdns BT4	22	U16
Eccles St BT13	19	J14
Edenbrook Cl BT13	19	J13
Eden Ct BT4	22	V15
Edenderry Cl BT13	19	J13
Edenderry Ct BT13	19	J13
Edenmore Dr BT11	24	C21
Edenvale Cres BT4	22	V15
Edenvale Dr BT4	22	U15
Edenvale Gdns BT4	22	U15
Edenvale Gro BT4	22	V15
Edenvale Pk BT4	22	U15
Edgar St BT5	21	Q16
Edgecumbe Dr BT4	22	V15
Edgecumbe Gdns BT4	22	V14
Edgecumbe Pk BT4	22	V14
Edgecumbe Vw BT4	22	V14
Edgewater Dr BT3	15	S8
Edgewater Rd BT3	15	R8
Edinburgh Av, Hol. BT18	11	BB7
Edinburgh Ms BT9	26	K19
Edinburgh St BT9	25	J19
Edith St BT5	21	R16
Edlingham St BT15	14	M12
Edwina St BT13		
off Riga St	19	J14
Egeria St BT12	19	K18
Eglantine Av BT9	26	K19
Eglantine Gdns BT9	26	L19
Eglantine Pl BT9	26	K19
Egmont Gdns BT12	30	A6
Eia St BT14	14	L12
Eileen Gdns BT9	26	K20
Elaine St BT9	26	M19
Elesington Ct BT6		
off Mayfair Av	27	S20
Elgin St BT7	26	N19
Elimgrove St BT14	14	K11
Elizabeth Rd, Hol. BT18	11	BB6
Eliza Pl BT7		
off Eliza St	31	F4
Eliza St BT7	31	F4
Eliza St Cl BT7	31	F4
Eliza St Ter BT7	31	F5
Elm Ct BT7	30	D6
Elmdale St BT5	21	T16
Elmfield St BT14	13	H12
Elmgrove Manor BT5	21	S17
Elmgrove Rd BT5	21	S17
Elm St BT7	30	D6
Elmwood Av BT9	20	L18
Elmwood Ms BT9	20	L18
Elsmere Hts BT5	29	AA19
Elsmere Manor BT5	29	AA19
Elsmere Pk BT5	29	AA19
Elswick St BT12	19	H15
Emerald St BT6	21	Q17
Empire Dr BT12	19	K17
Empire Par BT12	19	K17
Empire St BT12	19	J17
Enfield Dr BT13	19	H13
Enfield Par BT13	19	H13
Enfield St BT13	19	H13
Enid Dr BT5	22	V16
Enid Par BT5	22	V16
Epworth St BT5	21	R16
Erin Way BT7	30	D5
Errigal Pk BT11	24	D21
Erris Gro BT11		
off Oranmore Dr	24	B23
Erskine St BT5	21	R16
Eskdale Gdns BT14	13	H11
Esmond St BT13		
off Shankill Rd	19	J14
Espie Way BT6	28	U20
Esplanade, The, Hol.		
BT18	11	Y6
Essex Gro BT7	20	N18
Esther St BT15	14	N11
Estoril Ct BT14	13	H12
Estoril Pk BT14	13	H12
Ethel St BT9	25	J20
Etna Dr BT14	13	H11
Eureka Dr BT12	30	A6
Euston Par BT6	21	R18
Euston St BT6	21	R17
Euterpe St BT12	19	K18
Evelyn Av BT5	21	T16
Evelyn Gdns BT15	14	L9
Eversleigh St BT6	21	Q17
Everton Dr BT6	27	S22
Evewilliam Pk BT15	14	L9
Evolina St BT15	14	M12
Exchange Pl BT1		
off Donegall St	31	E1
Exchange St W BT1	20	N14
Excise Wk BT12	19	K16

F

Street	Map	Grid
Faburn Pk BT14	13	G10
Factory St BT5		
off East Bread St	21	S16
Fairfax Ct BT14	14	K12
Fairhill Gdns BT15	9	M7
Fairhill Pk BT15	9	M7
Fairhill Wk BT15	9	M7
Fairhill Way BT15	9	M7
Fairway Gdns BT5	29	X20
Falcon Rd BT12	25	J20
Falcon Way BT12		
off Falcon Rd	25	J20
Falls Ct BT13		
off Conway Link	19	J15
Falls Rd BT11	25	F19
Falls Rd BT12	18	F18
Fallswater Dr BT12		
off Falls Rd	19	H17
Fallswater St BT12	19	H17
Fane St BT9	19	K18
Farmhill Rd, Hol. BT18	11	BB4
Farmhurst Grn BT5	29	Y19
Farmhurst Way BT5	29	Y19
Farnham St BT7	20	N18
Farringdon Ct BT14	13	H11
Farringdon Gdns BT14	13	H11
Fashoda St BT5	21	S17
Federation St BT6	21	Q18
Felt St BT12	30	A6
Ferguson Dr BT4	22	U15
Ferndale Ct BT9	25	J20
Ferndale St BT9	25	J20
Fernhill Gro BT13	13	F11
Fernhill Hts BT13	13	F12
Fern St BT4		
off Frome St	21	R15
Fernvale St BT4	22	U14
Fernwood St BT7	26	N20
Fife St BT15	14	N11
Fifth St BT13	19	K15
Finaghy Pk Cen BT10	24	D24
Finaghy Pk N BT10	24	E23
Finaghy Pk S BT10	24	E24
Finaghy Rd N BT10	24	E23
Finaghy Rd N BT11	24	D21
Finaghy Rd S BT10	24	E24
Finbank Ct BT9	25	G24
Finbank Gdns BT9	25	G24
Finch Cl BT9	25	H24
Finch Ct BT9		
off Finch Way	25	H24
Finch Gro BT9	25	H24
Finchley Dr BT4	22	X13
Finchley Gdns BT4		
off Finchley Pk	22	X13
Finchley Pk BT4	22	X13
Finchley Vale BT4	22	X13
Finch Pl BT9		
off Finch Gro	25	H24
Finch Way BT9	25	H24
Findon Gdns BT9	25	G24
Findon Gro BT9	25	H24
Findon Pl BT9	25	H24
Fingals Ct BT13	30	A1
Fingal St BT13	19	H13
Finlay Pk, New. BT36	9	N4
Finmore Ct BT4	21	R15
Finnis Cl BT9	25	G24
Finnis Dr BT9	25	G24
Finn Sq BT13	30	A1
Finsbury St BT6	27	R19
Finvoy St BT5	21	T16
Finwood Ct BT9	25	G24
Finwood Pk BT9	25	G24
Firmount BT15	14	L9
Firmount Ct, Hol.		
BT18	17	Z9
Firmount Cres, Hol.		
BT18	17	Z9
First St BT13	19	K15
Fisherwick Pl BT1		
off College Sq E	30	C3
Fitzroy Av BT7	20	M18
Fitzroy Ct BT7		
off Fitzroy Av	20	M18
Fitzwilliam Av BT7	27	P21
Fitzwilliam Sq BT7	20	N18
Fitzwilliam St BT9	20	L18
Flaxcentre BT14	13	J12
Flax St BT14	13	J12
Flaxton Pl BT14		
off Old Mill Rd	12	E9
Fleetwood St BT14		
off Crumlin Rd	20	L13
Flora St BT5	21	S17
Flora St Walkway BT5	21	S17
Florence Ct BT13	20	L13
Florence Pl BT13	20	L13
Florence Sq BT13	20	L13
Florenceville Av BT7	27	P21
Florenceville Dr BT7	27	P21
Florence Wk BT13		
off Hopewell Av	20	L13
Florida Dr BT6	21	Q18
Florida St BT6	21	Q17
Flush Dr BT6	27	Q21
Flush Gdns BT6	27	Q21
Flush Grn BT6	27	Q21
Flush Pk BT6	27	Q21
Flush Rd BT14	12	D7
Fodnamona Ct BT11		
off Aitnamona Cres	24	D19
Forest Hill BT9	26	K23
Forest St BT12	19	H15
Forfar La BT12	19	H15
Forfar St BT12	19	H15
Forfar Way BT12	19	H15
Formby Pk BT14	13	H9
Forster St BT13		
off Ariel St	19	K14
Forsythe St BT13		
off Dover Pl	20	L14
Fortfield BT15	14	M12
Forthbrook Ct BT13		
off Ballygomartin Rd	18	F13
Forth Par BT13	19	H14
Forthriver Cl BT13	12	E11
Forthriver Cotts BT14		
off Ballysillan Rd	8	J8
Forthriver Cres BT13	13	F11
Forthriver Dale BT13	12	E11
Forthriver Dr BT13	13	F11
Forthriver Grn BT13	12	E11
Forthriver Link BT13	13	F11
Forthriver Par BT13	12	E11
Forthriver Pk BT13	12	E10
Forthriver Pas BT13	18	F13
Forthriver Rd BT13	12	E11
Forthriver Way BT13	13	F12
Fort St BT12	19	H15
Fortuna St BT12	19	K18
Fortwilliam Ct BT15		
off Fortwilliam Pk	14	L9
Fortwilliam Cres BT15	14	N9

Fortwilliam Demesne
  BT15 **9** M8
Fortwilliam Dr BT15 **8** L8
Fortwilliam Gdns BT15 **14** L9
Fortwilliam Gra BT15 **9** N8
Fortwilliam Par BT15 **14** M9
Fortwilliam Pk BT15 **14** L9
Fountain La BT1 **30** D2
Fountain St BT1 **30** D2
Fountain St N BT15
  off New Lo Rd **20** M13
Fountainville Av BT9 **20** L18
Four Winds Dr BT8 **27** S24
Four Winds Pk BT8 **27** S24
Foxglove St BT5 **21** S17
Foyle Ct BT14 **19** K13
Francis St BT1 **30** C1
Franklin St BT2 **30** C3
Franklin St Pl BT2
  off Franklin St **30** D4
Frank Pl BT5
  off Castlereagh St **21** S16
Frank St BT5 **21** R16
Fraser Pass BT4
  off Wolff Cl **21** Q15
Fraser St BT3 **21** Q14
Frederick La BT1
  off Frederick St **20** M14
Frederick Pl BT1
Frederick St BT1 **20** M14
Frenchpark St BT12 **19** J18
Friendly Pl BT7 **31** G4
Friendly Row BT7 **31** F4
Friendly St BT7 **31** F4
Friendly Way BT7 **31** F4
Frome St BT4 **21** R15
Fruithill Ct BT11 **24** E20
Fruithill Pk BT11 **24** E19
Fulton St BT7 **30** C6

G

Gaffikin St BT12 **30** B6
Gainsborough Dr BT15 **14** M11
Galwally Av BT8 **27** P23
Galwally Pk BT8 **27** Q22
Galway St BT12 **30** B2
Gamble St BT1 **20** N14
Gardenmore BT15
  off Salisbury Av **8** L8
Gardiner Pl BT13 **20** L14
Gardiner St BT13 **30** B1
Garland Av BT8 **27** S24
Garland Cres BT8 **27** S24
Garland Grn BT8 **27** S24
Garland Hill BT8 **27** S24
Garland Pk BT8 **27** S24
Garmoyle St BT15 **20** N13
Garnerville Dr BT4 **17** X12
Garnerville Gdns BT4 **17** X12
Garnerville Gro BT4 **17** X12
Garnerville Pk BT4 **17** X12
Garnerville Rd BT4 **17** X12
Garnock BT11 **24** C23
Garnock Hill BT10 **24** C24
Garnock Hill Pk BT10 **24** C24
Garranard Manor BT4 **22** W14
Garranard Pk BT4 **22** W14
Garron Cres BT10 **25** F24
Gartree Pl BT11 **24** C20
Gawn St BT4 **21** S15
Geary Rd BT5 **29** Z19
Geeragh Pl BT10 **25** F24
Geneva Gdns BT9 **26** M21
Genoa St BT12 **19** K16
Geoffrey St BT13 **19** J13
Ghent Pl BT13
  off Sydney St W **19** J13
Gibson Pk Av BT6 **27** S19
Gibson Pk Dr BT6
  off Cregagh Rd
Gibson Pk Gdns BT6 **21** R18
Gibson St BT12 **19** K16
Gilbourne Ct BT5 **29** Y19
Gilnahirk Av BT5 **29** Y19
Gilnahirk Cres BT5 **29** Y19
Gilnahirk Dr BT5 **29** Y19
Gilnahirk Pk BT5 **29** Y19

Gilnahirk Ri BT5 **29** Y19
Gilnahirk Rd BT5 **23** Y17
Gilnahirk Rd W BT5 **29** AA20
Gilnahirk Wk BT5 **29** Y19
Gipsy St BT7 **27** P20
Glandore Av BT15 **14** L10
Glandore Dr BT15 **14** L10
Glandore Gdns BT15 **14** L9
Glandore Par BT15
  off Ashfield Gdns **14** M10
Glanleam Dr BT15 **14** M10
Glantane Dr BT15 **14** L10
Glantrasna Dr BT15 **14** M10
Glanworth Dr BT15 **14** L10
Glanworth Gdns BT15 **14** L10
Glasgow St BT15 **14** N11
Glassmullin Gdns BT11 **24** D21
Glastonbury Av BT15 **8** L7
Glen, The BT15 **14** M11
Glenalina Cres BT12 **18** E17
Glenalina Gdns BT12
  off Glenalina Cres **18** E17
Glenalina Grn BT12
  off Glenalina Rd **18** E16
Glenalina Pk BT12 **18** E16
Glenalina Pas BT12
  off Glenalina Rd **18** E16
Glenalina Rd BT12 **18** E16
Glenallen St BT5 **21** R16
Glenard Brook BT14 **14** K11
Glenbank Dr BT14 **13** F10
Glenbank Par BT14
  off Leroy St **13** F10
Glenbank Pl BT14 **13** F10
Glenbrook Av BT5 **21** T17
Glenbryn Dr BT14 **13** H11
Glenbryn Gdns BT14 **13** G11
Glenbryn Par BT14 **13** G11
Glenbryn Pk BT14 **13** H11
Glenburn Pk BT14 **14** K9
Glencairn Cres BT13 **13** G12
Glencairn Pas BT13 **12** E11
Glencairn Rd BT13 **12** E11
Glencairn St BT13 **13** G12
Glencairn Wk BT13 **12** E11
Glencairn Way BT13 **12** E11
Glencoe Pk, New. BT36 **8** L4
Glencollyer St BT15 **14** M11
Glencourt BT11 **25** F19
Glencregagh Ct BT6 **27** Q23
Glencregagh Dr BT6 **27** R23
Glencregagh Pk BT6 **27** R23
Glencregagh Rd BT8 **27** R23
Glen Cres BT11 **25** F19
Glendale BT10 **24** C24
Glendale Av E BT8 **27** R24
Glendale Av N BT8 **27** Q24
Glendale Av S BT8 **27** R24
Glendale Av W BT8 **27** R24
Glendarragh BT4 **17** X11
Glendarragh Ms BT4 **17** X10
Glendhu Grn BT4 **17** X12
Glendhu Gro BT4 **16** W12
Glendhu Manor BT4 **16** W11
Glendhu Pk BT4 **17** X11
Glendower St BT6 **27** R19
Glen Ebor Hts BT4
  off Glenmachan Rd **17** Y12
Glen Ebor Pk BT4 **17** Y12
Glenfarne St BT13
  off Agnes St **19** K13
Glengall La BT12
Glengall Ms BT12
  off Glengall St **30** C4
Glengall St BT12 **30** B4
Glenhill Ct BT14
  off Glenpark St **14** K12
Glenhill Pk BT11 **24** E19
Glenholm Av BT8 **27** R24
Glenholm Cres BT8 **27** R24
Glenholm Pk BT8 **27** R24
Glenhoy Dr BT5 **21** T17
Glenhoy Ms BT5 **21** T17
Glenhurst Ct, New.
  BT36 **9** M4
Glenhurst Dr, New.
  BT36 **9** M4

Glenhurst Gdns, New.
  BT36 **9** M4
Glenhurst Par, New.
  BT36 **9** M4
Glenlea Gro BT4 **17** X11
Glenlea Pk BT4 **17** X12
Glenloch Gdns BT4 **17** X11
Glenluce Dr BT4 **17** X12
Glenluce Grn BT4 **17** X11
Glenluce Wk BT4 **17** X11
Glenmachan Av BT4 **23** Y13
Glenmachan Dr BT4 **23** Y13
Glenmachan Gro BT4 **23** Y13
Glenmachan Ms BT4 **23** Y13
Glenmachan Pk BT4 **17** Y12
Glenmachan Pl BT12 **19** H18
Glenmachan Rd BT4 **17** Y12
Glenmachan St BT12 **19** J18
Glen Manor BT11 **24** E19
Glenmillan Dr BT4 **17** X12
Glenmillan Pk BT4 **22** X13
Glenmore St BT5 **21** R16
Glenmurry Ct BT11
  off Glen Rd **24** E19
Glen Par BT11 **25** F19
Glenpark Ct BT14
  off Glenpark St **13** J12
Glenpark St BT14 **13** J12
Glenravel St BT15
  off Henry Pl **20** M13
Glen Ri BT5 **28** W19
Glen Rd BT4 **23** Z13
Glen Rd BT5 **28** V19
Glen Rd BT11 **24** E19
Glen Rd BT12
  off Falls Rd **24** E19
Glen Rd Hts BT11 **24** B19
Glenrosa Link BT15
  off Glenrosa St **14** N12
Glenrosa St BT15 **14** M12
Glenrosa St S BT15
  off Duncairn Gdns **14** M12
Glenshane Gdns BT11 **24** D21
Glensharragh Av BT6 **28** T21
Glensharragh Gdns
  BT6 **28** T20
Glensharragh Pk BT6 **28** T21
Glenside BT14 **13** F10
Glenside Par BT14 **13** F10
Glenside Pk BT14 **13** F11
Glentilt St BT13
  off Agnes St **19** K13
Glentoran Pl BT6
  off Mount St S **21** Q17
Glentoran St BT6
  off Mount St S **21** Q17
Glenvale St BT13 **19** H13
Glenvarloch St BT5 **21** S17
Glenview Av BT5 **28** W20
Glenview Ct BT5
  off Glenview St **14** K12
Glenview Cres BT5 **28** V21
Glenview Dr BT5
  off Glenview Gdns **28** W20
Glenview Gdns BT5 **28** W20
Glenview Hts BT5 **28** V20
Glenview Pk BT5 **28** V20
Glenview Rd, Hol. BT18 **11** BB7
Glenview St BT14 **14** K12
Glenview Ter BT11 **24** B22
Glenwherry Pl BT6
  off Mount St S **21** Q17
Glenwood Pl BT13
  off Glenwood St **19** J14
Glenwood St BT13 **19** J14
Gloucester St BT1 **31** E3
Gordon St BT1 **20** N14
Gortfin St BT12 **19** H16
Gortgrib Dr BT5 **29** Z19
Gortin Dr BT5 **23** Z17
Gortin Pk BT5 **23** Z17
Gortland Av BT5 **29** Z19
Gortland Pk BT5 **29** Z19
Gortnamona Ct BT11
  off Gortnamona Way **18** D18
Gortnamona Hts BT11
  off Gortnamona Way **18** D18

Gortnamona Pl BT11
  off Gortnamona Way **18** D18
Gortnamona Ri BT11
  off Gortnamona Way **18** D18
Gortnamona Vw BT11
  off Gortnamona Way **18** D18
Gortnamona Way
  BT11 **18** D18
Gotha St BT6 **21** Q17
Govan Dr BT5 **23** AA18
Governor's Br, The BT7 **26** M20
Governor's Br, The BT9 **26** M20
Grace Av BT5 **21** T17
Gracehill Ct BT14 **14** K12
Grace St BT2 **31** E4
Grafton St BT13
  off Beresford St **19** K14
Graham Gdns BT6 **27** S19
Grampian Av BT4 **21** T16
Grampian Cl BT4 **21** T15
Grampian St BT4 **21** T15
Grand Par BT5 **21** T18
Grange, The BT4 **23** Y13
Grangeville Dr BT10
  off Grangeville Gdns **24** E23
Grangeville Gdns BT10 **24** E23
Gransha Av BT11 **24** E19
Gransha Cres BT11 **24** E19
Gransha Dr BT11 **24** E19
Gransha Gdns BT11 **18** E18
Gransha Grn BT11 **18** E18
Gransha Gro BT11 **24** E19
Gransha Par BT11 **24** E19
Gransha Pk BT11 **18** E18
Gransha Ri BT11 **18** E18
Gransha Way BT11 **24** E19
Granton Pk BT5 **23** AA17
Granville Pl BT12
  off Servia St **19** K16
Grasmere Gdns BT15 **8** K8
Graymount Cres, New.
  BT36 **9** N5
Graymount Dr, New.
  BT36 **9** N5
Graymount Gdns, New.
  BT36 **9** N5
Graymount Gro, New.
  BT36 **9** N5
Graymount Par, New.
  BT36 **9** N5
Graymount Pk, New.
  BT36 **9** N5
Graymount Rd, New.
  BT36 **9** N5
Graymount Ter, New.
  BT36 **9** N5
Grays Ct BT15 **9** N5
Grays La BT15 **9** M5
Grays La, Hol. BT18
  off High St **11** Z6
Great Georges St BT15 **20** M13
Great Northern St BT9 **25** J20
Great Patrick St BT1 **20** M14
Great Victoria St BT2 **30** C4
Green, The, Hol. BT18 **11** Z8
Greenan BT11
  off Rossnareen Rd **24** C20
Greenan Av BT11 **24** C21
Greenan Cres BT10 **24** C23
Greenan Dr BT10 **24** C23
Greencastle Cl, New.
  BT36 **9** N5
Greencastle St BT13 **9** N6
Green Cres BT5 **22** W16
Greenhill Gro BT14
  off Wolfend Dr **13** F9
Greenhill La BT14 **13** F9
Greenland St BT13 **20** L14
Greenlea Gdns BT5
  off Whincroft Rd **28** W19
Green Mt BT5 **28** W19
Greenmount Pl BT15
  off Glenrosa St **14** N12
Greenmount St BT15
  off North Queen St **14** N12
Greenore St BT6 **21** R18
Green Rd BT5 **22** W16
Greenview Pk BT9 **25** H24

Street	No.	Grid
Greenville Av BT5	21	T16
Greenville Ct BT5		
off Woodcot Av	21	T17
Greenville Rd BT5	21	T17
Greenville St BT5	21	T16
Greenway BT6		
off North Bk	27	S20
Greenwich Ms BT10	25	G23
Greenwood Av BT4	22	W16
Greenwood Manor BT4		
off Greenwood Av	22	W16
Greenwood Pk BT4	22	W16
Gregg's Quay BT5	31	G2
Gresham St BT1	30	C1
Grey Castle Manor BT6	28	V21
Grillagh Way BT6	27	R21
Groomsport Ct BT14		
off Groomsport St	14	K12
Groomsport St BT14	14	K12
Grosvenor Arc BT12		
off Roden Pas	19	K16
Grosvenor Ct BT12		
off Selby Ct	19	K16
Grosvenor Rd BT12	19	J16
Grove, The, Hol. BT18	11	Z8
Grove Ct BT15	14	N11
Grovefield Pl BT6		
off Grovefield St	21	Q17
Grovefield St BT6	21	Q16
Grove Pl BT15	14	N11
Grove St BT7	20	N18
Grove St E BT5	21	R17
Grove Tree N BT12		
off Devonshire St	30	A3
Grove Tree S BT12		
off Devonshire St	30	A3
Gunnell Hill, New. BT36	9	M4
H		
Haddington Gdns BT6	27	R19
Haig St BT5	21	R16
Halcombe St BT6	21	Q17
Halfpenny Ms BT5	21	S17
Hallidays Rd BT15	14	M12
Halstein Dr BT5	22	V16
Hamel Dr BT6	27	S21
Hamel Ms BT6		
off Hamel Dr	27	S21
Hamill Glen BT11	24	C20
Hamill Gro BT11	24	C20
Hamill Pk BT11	24	C20
Hamill St BT12	30	B2
Hamilton Pl BT6		
off Swift St	21	Q16
Hamilton St BT3	21	Q13
Hamiltons Ct BT1		
off High St	31	E1
Hamilton St BT2	31	E4
Hamlets, The BT4	22	X16
Hampton Ct, Hol. BT18	11	BB6
Hampton Dr BT7	26	N20
Hampton Gdns BT7		
off Hampton Dr	26	N20
Hampton Gro BT7		
off Hampton Par	26	M20
Hampton Manor BT7	27	P22
Hampton Manor Dr BT7	26	N22
Hampton Par BT7	26	M20
Hampton Pk BT7	27	P23
Hampton Pl BT7		
off Hampton Dr	26	N20
Hampton Strand BT7		
off Hampton Dr	26	N20
Hanna St BT15	14	N12
Harberton Av BT9	25	H23
Harberton Dr BT9	25	H23
Harberton Pk BT9	25	H23
Harcourt Dr BT14	14	K12
Hardcastle St BT7	30	D5
Hardinge Pl BT15		
off New Lo Rd	20	M13
Harkness Par BT4	35	S14
Harland Cl BT4	21	R15
Harland Dr BT4	21	R15
Harland Pk BT4	21	T15
Harland Tech Pk BT3	21	R14
Harland Wk BT4		
off Pitt Pl	21	Q15
Harleston St BT9	26	M21
Harmony BT14		
off Glenbank Dr	13	F10
Harmony St BT2	30	C5
Harpers Ct BT1		
off Curtis St	20	N14
Harper St BT5	21	Q16
Harrisburg St BT15	14	N10
Harrison Wk BT13		
off Danube St	19	J13
Harrogate St BT12	19	H16
Harrow St BT7	26	N19
Hartington St BT7		
off Dublin Rd	30	C6
Hartwell Pl BT15	14	M12
Harvey Ct BT5	21	R16
Hatfield St BT7	20	N18
Hatton Dr BT6	21	R17
Havana Ct BT14	13	J12
Havana Gdns BT14	13	J12
Havana Wk BT14		
off Ardoyne Av	13	J12
Havana Way BT14		
off Ardoyne Av	13	J12
Havelock St BT7	31	E6
Hawthornden Ct BT4	22	X16
Hawthornden Dr BT4	22	X14
Hawthornden Gdns BT4	22	X15
Hawthornden Gate BT4	22	X15
Hawthornden Lo BT4	22	X15
Hawthornden Ms BT4	22	X16
Hawthornden Pk BT4	22	X16
Hawthornden Rd BT4	22	X15
Hawthornden Way BT4	22	X15
Hawthorn St BT12	19	J16
Haymarket BT1		
off Gresham St	30	C1
Haypark Av BT7	26	N21
Haypark Gdns BT7	26	N21
Haywood Av BT7	26	N20
Haywood Dr BT7	26	N20
Hazelbank Ct BT5	23	Y17
Hazelbrook Dr BT14	13	F9
Hazelfield St BT13	19	K13
Hazelnut St BT14	14	K12
Heatherbell St BT5	21	S17
Heather St BT13	19	H13
Heathfield Ct BT14		
off Torrens Rd	14	K11
Heathfield Dr BT14	13	J11
Heathfield Rd BT14	14	K11
Heath Lo Av BT13	18	E14
Heath Lo Cl BT13	18	E14
Heath Lo Dr BT13	18	E14
Heath Lo Ms BT13	18	E14
Heath Lo Sq BT13	18	E14
Helens Lea BT5	29	Z19
Helgor Pk BT4	22	V14
Helgor Pk Ms BT4	22	W14
Henderson Av BT15	8	K8
Henderson Av Flats BT15	8	K8
Henderson Ct BT15		
off Henderson Av	8	K8
Henderson Cr, Hol. BT18	17	X11
Henrietta St BT2	31	E4
Henry Pl BT15	20	M13
Henry St BT15	20	M13
Herat St BT7	26	N19
Herbert St BT14	13	H12
Herdman Channel Rd BT3	15	Q10
Heron Av BT3	10	V8
Heron Rd BT3	10	V8
Herrons Row BT13		
off Beresford St	19	K14
Hesketh Gdns BT13	13	G11
Hesketh Pk BT14	13	G11
Hesketh Rd BT14	13	G11
Hewitt Par BT5	22	V16
Hibernia St, Hol. BT18	11	Z6
Highburn Cres BT13	18	F14
Highburn Gdns BT13	18	F14
Highbury Gdns BT14	13	H12
Highcairn Dr BT13	18	F14
Highcliff Gdns BT13	18	F14
Highdene Gdns BT13	18	F14
Highfern Gdns BT13	18	F14
Highfield Dr BT13	18	F15
Highgate BT13		
off West Circular Rd	18	F14
Highgate Ter BT13		
off Highfield Dr	18	F14
Highgreen BT13	18	F14
Highland Par BT13	18	F14
High Link BT13	18	F15
Highpark Cres BT13	18	F15
Highpark Cross BT13		
off Highpark Dr	18	F15
Highpark Dr BT13	18	F14
High Pass BT13	18	F15
High Side BT13		
off Highfield Dr	18	F15
High St BT1	31	E2
High St, Hol. BT18	11	Z6
High St, New. BT36	9	N4
High St Ct BT1		
off High St	31	E1
Highvale Gdns BT13	18	F14
Highview Cres BT13	18	F14
Highway BT13	18	F14
Hillburn Pk BT6	28	T21
Hillcrest Gdns BT5	22	U17
Hillfoot St BT4	21	T15
Hillhead Av BT11	24	C21
Hillhead Cotts BT11	24	C21
Hillhead Ct BT11	24	C21
Hillhead Cres BT11	24	C22
Hillhead Dr BT11	24	C22
Hillhead Hts BT11	24	C21
Hillhead Pk BT11	24	C21
Hillman Cl BT15	14	M12
Hillman Ct BT15	14	M12
Hillman St BT15	14	M12
Hills Av BT4	21	T14
Hillsborough Dr BT6	21	R18
Hillsborough Gdns BT6	21	R18
Hillsborough Par BT6	21	S18
Hillside Cres BT9	26	L22
Hillside Dr BT9	26	L22
Hillside Gdns BT9	26	L22
Hillside Pk BT6	28	V20
Hillside Pk BT9	26	L22
Hill St BT1	20	N14
Hill St Ms, Hol. BT18	11	Z6
Hillview Av BT5	22	V16
Hillview Ct BT14	14	K12
Hillview Pl, Hol. BT18	11	AA6
Hillview Retail Pk BT14	13	J12
Hillview Rd BT14	13	J12
Hindsdale Pk BT6	27	S21
Hogarth St BT15	14	M12
Holland Cres BT5	22	V16
Holland Dr BT5	22	V17
Holland Gdns BT5	22	V17
Holland Pk BT5	22	V17
Hollies, The BT5	22	U16
Hollycroft Av BT5	21	T16
Holmdene Gdns BT14	13	H11
Holmes St BT2	30	C4
Holyrood BT9	26	L20
Holywood Bypass, Hol. BT18	11	Y8
Holywood Rd BT4	21	T15
Holywood Rd, Hol. BT18	22	W13
Hopedene Ct BT4		
off Dundela Gdns	22	U15
Hopedene Ms BT4		
off Dundela Av	22	U15
Hopefield Av BT15	14	L10
Hopefield Ct BT15	14	L10
Hope St BT12	30	B4
Hopewell Av BT13	19	K13
Hopewell Cres BT13	20	L14
Hopewell Pl BT13	20	L14
Hopewell Sq BT13	20	L14
Hornby Cres BT5	21	S15
Hornby Par BT5		
off Hornby St	21	R15
Hornby St BT5	21	S16
Horn Dr BT11	24	B22
Horn Wk BT11	24	B22
Horseshoe Ct BT14	13	F8
Houston Ct BT5	22	V16
Houston Dr BT5	28	U19
Houston Gdns BT5	22	U18
Houston Pk BT5	28	U19
Howard St BT1	30	C3
Hoylake Pk BT14	13	H9
Huddlestons Pl BT5		
off Seaforde St	21	Q15
Hudson Pl BT13		
off North Boundary St	20	L14
Hughenden Av BT15	14	L9
Hughes Ct BT6	27	R21
Hugh St BT9	25	J21
Hugo St BT12	19	G18
Humber Ct BT4	21	S15
Humber St BT4		
off Severn St	21	S15
Humes Ct BT15		
off Ludlow Sq	20	M13
Hunter Pk BT12	30	A6
Hurst Pk BT12		
off Linfield Rd	30	B5
Huss St BT13		
off Huss Row	19	K14
Huss Row BT13	19	K14
Hutchison St BT12	30	A3
Hyndford St BT5	21	S17
I		
Ilchester St BT15	14	M12
Imperial Dr BT6	21	Q18
Imperial St BT6	21	Q18
Ina St BT4	21	R15
Indiana Av BT15	14	L9
India St BT7	20	M18
Ingledale Pk BT14	13	G12
Inglewood Ct BT4		
off Station Rd	22	U13
Inishmore Cres BT11	24	C21
Innes Pl BT12	30	B6
Innis Ct, Hol. BT18		
off High St	11	Z6
Innisfayle Dr BT15	9	M7
Innisfayle Gdns BT15	9	N6
Innisfayle Pk BT15	8	L7
Innisfayle Pas BT15	9	N6
Innisfayle Rd BT15	9	M7
Institution Pl BT12	30	B2
Inverary Av BT4	22	V13
Inverary Dr BT4	22	U13
Inverary Wd BT4	22	U13
Inver Av BT15	14	K9
Inveresk Par BT4	22	V13
Inverleith Dr BT4	22	U13
Invernook Dr BT4	22	U13
Invernook Pk BT4	22	U13
Inver Pk, Hol. BT18	11	AA7
Inverwood Ct BT4	22	V13
Inverwood Gdns BT4	22	V13
Ireton St BT7	20	M18
Iris Cl BT12	19	H16
Iris Dr BT12	19	H16
Iris Gro BT12	19	H16
Iris Ms BT12	19	H16
Iris St BT12	19	H16
Iris Wk BT12	19	H16
Irwell Ct BT12	19	J17
Irwin Av BT4	21	T16
Irwin Cres BT4	22	U15
Irwin Dr BT4	21	T16
Isaacs Ct BT12		
off Sandy Row	30	B5
Isadore Av BT13	19	G15
Islandbawn Dr BT12		
off Falls Rd	19	H17
Islandbawn St BT12	19	H17
Island St BT4	21	R15
Isoline St BT5	21	S17
Isthmus St BT6	21	R17
Ivan Cl BT15	14	N11
Ivan St BT15	14	N11
Iveagh Cres BT12	19	H17
Iveagh Dr BT12	19	H17

Iveagh Par BT12	19	H17	Kerrera Ms BT14			Kinnegar Rd BT10	25	F24	Ladybrook Av BT11	24	C22
Iveagh St BT12	19	H17	*off Kerrera St*	13	H12	Kinnegar Rd, Hol.			Ladybrook Cres BT11	24	C22
Iverna Cl BT12	19	K17	Kerrera St BT14	13	H12	BT18	11	Y6	Ladybrook Cross BT11	24	C23
Iverna St BT12	19	K17	Kerrington Ct BT9			Kinross Av BT5	23	AA17	Ladybrook Dr BT11	24	D22
			off Marlborough Pk S	26	K21	Kirk Cres BT13			Ladybrook Gdns BT11	24	D22
J			Kerrsland Cres BT5	22	V16	*off Kirk St*	19	H15	Ladybrook Gro BT11	24	D22
Jacksons Rd, Hol. BT18	11	Y8	Kerrsland Dr BT5	22	V16	Kirkliston Dr BT5	22	U16	Ladybrook Par BT11	24	C22
Jackson St BT13			Kerrsland Ms BT5	22	V16	Kirkliston Gdns BT5	22	V17	Ladybrook Pk BT11	24	C22
off North			Kerrsland Par BT5	22	V16	Kirkliston Pk BT5	22	U17	Ladymar Ct BT12		
Boundary St	20	L14	Keswick St BT13	19	J13	Kirklowe Dr BT10	24	E24	*off Lady St*	19	K16
Jamaica Ct BT14	13	J11	Keylands Pl BT2			Kirk St BT13	19	H14	Ladymar Gro BT12		
Jamaica Rd BT14	13	J11	*off Amelia St*	30	C4	Kirn Pk BT5	23	AA18	*off Lady St*	19	K16
Jamaica St BT14	13	J11	Kilbroney Bend BT6	27	S21	Kitchener Dr BT12	19	J18	Ladymar Pk BT12		
Jamaica Way BT14	13	J11	Kilburn St BT12	19	J18	Kitchener St BT12	19	J18	*off Lady St*	19	K16
James Ct BT15			Kilcoole Gdns BT14	8	H7	Klondyke St BT13	19	K14	Ladymar Wk BT12		
off Kansas Av Flats	14	L10	Kilcoole Pk BT14	8	H7	Knightsbridge Manor			*off Lady St*	19	K16
Jameson St BT7	27	P20	Kildare Pl BT13	20	M14	BT9	26	L23	Ladymar Way BT12		
James's Pas BT7			Kildare St BT13	20	M14	Knightsbridge Ms BT9	26	L22	*off Lady St*	19	K16
off Ormeau Rd	31	E6	Kilhorne Gdns BT5	22	X18	Knightsbridge Pk BT9	26	L23	Lady St BT12	19	K16
James St S BT2	30	C4	Killagan Bend BT6	27	R20	Knights Grn BT6	27	S19	Laganbank Rd BT1	31	G3
Jellicoe Av BT15	14	M11	Killard Pl BT10	25	F24	Knockbracken Pk BT6	27	Q22	Lagan Br BT1	20	P14
Jellicoe Dr BT15	14	M10	Killarn Cl BT6	28	U20	Knockbreda Dr BT6	27	Q22	Lagan Br BT3	20	P14
Jellicoe Par BT15	14	N10	Killeen Pk BT11	24	D21	Knockbreda Gdns BT6	27	Q22	Laganvale Ct BT9	26	M22
Jellicoe Pk BT15	14	M10	Killowen St BT6	21	R18	Knockbreda Pk BT6	27	Q22	Laganvale Manor BT9	26	M22
Jennymount St BT15	14	N11	Kilmakee Pk BT5	29	AA19	Knockbreda Pk Ms BT6	27	Q22	Laganvale St BT9	26	M21
Jersey Pl BT13			Kilmore Cl BT13	19	J15	Knockbreda Rd BT6	27	P22	Laganview Ct BT5	31	G2
off Jersey St	19	K13	Kilmore Sq BT13	19	J15	Knockburn Pk BT5	23	Z16	Laganview Ms BT5	31	G2
Jersey St BT13	19	K13	Kilmory Gdns BT5	23	AA18	Knockcastle Pk BT5	22	X18	Lake Glen Av BT11	25	F19
Jerusalem St BT7	26	N19	Kimberley Dr BT7	26	N21	Knockdarragh Pk BT4	23	Y13	Lake Glen Cl BT11	25	F19
Jetty Rd BT3	16	U9	Kimberley St BT7	26	N20	Knockdene Pk BT5	22	X17	Lake Glen Cres BT11	24	E19
Joanmount Dr BT14	13	H9	Kimona Dr BT4	21	T14	Knockdene Pk N BT5	22	X16	Lake Glen Dr BT11	25	F19
Joanmount Gdns BT14	13	H9	Kimona St BT4	21	T14	Knockdene Pk S BT5	22	X16	Lake Glen Grn BT11	25	F19
Joanmount Pk BT14	13	H9	Kimscourt BT5	22	X18	Knockdhu Rd BT11	24	C20	Lake Glen Par BT11		
Jocelyn Av BT6	21	R17	Kinallen Ct BT7	26	N19	Knock Eden Cres BT6	27	Q21	*off Lake Glen Dr*	25	F19
Jocelyn Gdns BT6	21	R17	Kinallen St BT7			Knock Eden Dr BT6	27	Q21	Lake Glen Pk BT11	24	E19
Jocelyn St BT6	21	R17	*off Kinallen Ct*	26	N19	Knock Eden Gro BT6	27	Q21	Lanark Way BT13	19	H14
Johnston Ct BT5	22	X16	Kinbane Way BT10	25	F24	Knock Eden Par BT6	27	Q21	Lancaster St BT15	20	M14
John St BT12	30	B2	Kincora Av BT4	22	V16	Knock Eden Pk BT6	27	Q21	Lancaster Ter BT15		
Jonesboro Pk BT5	21	S17	Kincora Ms BT4	22	V16	Knock Grn BT5	28	W19	*off Lancaster St*	20	M14
Joys Entry BT1			Kincraig Av BT5	23	AA18	Knock Gro BT5	28	V19	Lancedean Rd BT6	27	S22
off Ann St	31	E2	Kinedar Cres BT4	22	W15	Knockhill Pk BT5	22	W16	Lancefield Rd BT9	25	J21
Joy St BT2	31	E5	Kingsberry Pk BT6	27	Q22	Knockland Pk BT5	23	Z17	Landscape Ter BT14	19	K13
Jubilee Av BT15	14	L11	Kings Brae BT5	23	Z17	Knock Link BT5	22	W18	Landseer St BT9	26	M19
Jubilee Rd BT9	20	L18	King's Br BT7	26	N20	Knocklofty Ct BT4	22	W15	Langholm Row BT5		
Jude St BT12	19	K15	King's Br BT9	26	N20	Knocklofty Pk BT4	22	W15	*off Granton Pk*	23	AA17
Julia St BT4	21	S15	Kings Ct BT10	25	G23	Knockmarloch Pk BT4	23	Y13	Langley St BT13		
			Kings Ct BT15			Knockmount Gdns BT5	22	W18	*off Tennent St*	19	J13
K			*off Lancaster St*	20	M14	Knockmount Pk BT5	22	W18	Langtry Ct BT5	21	R16
Kane St BT13	19	J15	Kingscourt Av BT6			Knocknagoney Av BT4	17	X11	Lansdowne Dr BT15	9	M8
Kansas Av BT15	14	L10	*off Euston St*	21	R17	Knocknagoney Dale			Lansdowne Ms BT15	9	M7
Kansas Av Flats BT15	14	L10	Kingscourt Cl BT6	21	R17	BT4			Lansdowne Pk BT15	9	M8
Kashmir Rd BT13	19	H15	Kingscourt Cres BT6	21	R17	*off Knocknagoney*			Lansdowne Pk N BT15	9	M7
Kathleen Ct BT5	21	R15	Kings Cres BT5	22	X17	*Rd*	16	W11	Lansdowne Rd BT15	9	M7
Keadyville Av BT15	14	N10	Kingsdale Pk BT5	23	Y17	Knocknagoney Dr BT4	17	X11	Lanyon Pl BT1	31	G3
Keatley St BT5	21	R16	Kingsden Pk BT5	22	W18	Knocknagoney Gdns			Larch Cl, Hol. BT18		
Kells Av BT11	24	B22	Kings Dr BT5	22	X17	BT4	17	X11	*off Loughview Av*	11	Z8
Kelvin Par BT14	14	K10	Kingsland Dr BT5	23	Z18	Knocknagoney Grn BT4	17	X11	Larch St BT5		
Kenard Av BT11	24	C20	Kingsland Pk BT5	23	Z18	Knocknagoney Gro BT4	17	X11	*off Trillick St*	21	R16
Kenbaan Ct BT5			Kingsleigh BT5	22	W17	Knocknagoney Pk BT4	16	W11	Larkfield Ct BT4		
off Trillick St	21	R16	Kingsley St BT4	22	V15	Knocknagoney Rd BT4	16	W11	*off Larkfield Rd*	22	U14
Kenbaan St BT5			Kings Link BT5	23	Z17	Knocknagoney Way			Larkfield Dr BT4	21	T13
off Beersbridge Rd	21	R17	Kings Manor BT5	23	Y17	BT4			Larkfield Gdns BT4	22	U13
Kenbella Par BT15			Kingsmere Av BT14	13	J10	*off Knocknagoney Av*	17	X11	Larkfield Gro BT4	22	U14
off Salisbury Av	14	L9	Kings Pk BT5	22	X17	Knock Rd BT5	28	V20	Larkfield Manor BT4	21	T14
Kendal St BT13	19	K14	Kings Pk La BT5	22	W17	Knocktern Gdns BT4	22	X16	Larkfield Pk BT4	22	U14
Kenilworth Pl BT4			Kings Rd BT5	22	W17	Knockvale Gro BT5	22	W17	Larkfield Rd BT4	22	U14
off Ballymacarrett			Kings Sq BT5	23	Y17	Knockvale Pk BT5	22	W17	Larkstone St BT9		
Rd	21	Q15	Kingston Ct BT14			Knock Way BT5	28	W19	*off Lisburn Rd*	25	H21
Kenmare Pk BT12	30	B5	*off Jamaica Rd*	13	J11	Knockwood Cres BT5	22	V18	La Salle Dr BT12	19	H17
Kennedy Way BT11	24	E19	King St BT1	30	C2	Knockwood Dr BT5	22	W18	La Salle Gdns BT12	19	H17
Kennel Br BT4	22	X13	King St Ms BT1	30	B2	Knockwood Gro BT5	22	W18	La Salle Ms BT12		
Kensington Av BT5	21	T17	Kings Vale BT5	22	W17	Knockwood Pk BT5	22	V18	*off La Salle Dr*	19	H17
Kensington Ct BT5	22	X18	Kingsway Av BT5	23	Y17	Knutsford Dr BT14	14	K10	La Salle Pk BT12	19	H17
Kensington Dr BT5	23	Y18	Kingsway Cl BT5	23	Y18	Koram Ring BT11			Laurelvale BT4	22	W15
Kensington Gdns BT5	22	X18	Kingsway Dr BT5	23	Y17	*off South Link*	24	E20	Laurel Wd BT8	26	N23
Kensington Gdns S BT5	22	X18	Kingsway Gdns BT5	23	Y18	Kylemore Pk BT14	8	J8	Lavens Dr BT14	13	F10
Kensington Gdns W			Kingsway Pk BT5	23	Y18	Kyle St BT4	21	T14	Lavinia Ms BT7	20	N18
BT5	22	X18	Kingswood Pk BT5	23	Z18				Lavinia Sq BT7	20	N18
Kensington Gate BT5	22	X18	Kingswood St BT5	21	R16	**L**			Lawnbrook Av BT13	19	J15
Kensington Manor BT5	23	Y18	Kinnaird Cl BT14	14	L12	Laburnum Ct BT5	21	T16	Lawnbrook Ct BT13	19	J15
Kensington Pk BT5	22	X18	Kinnaird Pl BT14	14	L12	Laburnum La BT5			Lawnbrook Dr BT13		
Kensington Rd BT5	22	X18	Kinnaird St BT14	20	L13	*off Bloomfield Av*	21	T16	*off Lawnbrook Av*	19	J14
Kensington St BT12	30	C6	Kinnaird Terrace BT14	20	L13	Laburnum St BT5	21	T16	Lawnbrook Sq BT13		
Kent St BT1	20	M14	Kinnaird Ter BT14			Lackagh Ct BT4	21	Q15	*off Lawnbrook Av*	19	J14
Kernan Cl, New. BT36			*off Kinnaird Pl*	20	L13	Ladas Dr BT6	27	S20	Lawnbrook Way BT13	19	J15
off Ballyroney Hill	9	M4	Kinnegar Av, Hol. BT18	11	Y6	Ladas Wk BT6	27	S19	Lawnmount St BT13	21	Q17
Kerrera Ct BT14			Kinnegar Ct, Hol. BT18	11	Y6	Ladas Way BT6	27	S19	Lawnview St BT13	19	H14
off Kerrera St	13	H12	Kinnegar Dr, Hol. BT18	11	Y6	Ladbrook Dr BT14	13	H12	Lawrence St BT7	20	M18

40

Laws Ct BT1 **20** M14
Lawther Ct BT15 **14** M11
Lawyer Gdns BT12
off Linfield Rd **30** B5
Lead Hill BT6 **28** V20
Lead Hill Pk BT6 **28** V20
Lead Hill Vw BT6 **28** V20
Lecale St BT12 **19** J18
Ledley Hall Cl BT5
off Beersbridge Rd **21** S17
Leeson St BT12 **19** K16
Leestone Ter BT11
off Kells Av **24** B22
Legann St BT14 **13** F10
Leganoe St BT14 **12** E9
Leggagh Ct BT14 **13** F10
Leginn St BT14 **12** E9
Legmail St BT14
off Crumlin Rd **13** F10
Legnavea St BT14 **12** E9
Legoniel Pl BT14 **12** E9
Leitrim St BT6 **21** R17
Lelia St BT4 **21** S15
Lemberg St BT12 **19** J17
Lemonfield Av, Hol. BT18 **11** AA7
Lenadoon Av BT11 **24** B21
Lenadoon Wk BT11 **24** B22
Lena St BT5 **21** T16
Lendrick St BT5 **21** R15
Lennox Av BT8 **27** Q24
Lennoxvale BT9 **26** L20
Leopold Gdns BT13 **19** H13
Leopold Pk BT13 **19** H13
Leopold Pl BT13 **19** J13
Leoville St BT13
off Kashmir Rd **19** H15
Lepper St BT15 **20** M13
Leroy St BT14 **13** F10
Leven Cl BT5
off Leven Dr **23** AA18
Leven Cres BT5 **23** AA18
Leven Dr BT5 **23** AA18
Leven Pk BT5 **23** AA18
Leven Pl BT5
off Leven Dr **23** AA18
Lever St BT14 **12** E8
Lewis Av BT4 **21** S15
Lewis Ct BT6 **21** R17
Lewis Dr BT4 **21** S15
Lewis Gdns BT4 **21** S15
Lewis Ms BT4 **21** S15
Lewis Pk BT4 **21** S15
Library Ct BT4 **22** W16
Library St BT1 **20** M14
Lichfield Av BT5 **21** T17
Liffey Ct BT14
off Shannon St **14** K12
Ligoniel Pl BT14 **12** E9
Ligoniel Rd BT14 **12** E8
Lille Pk BT10 **24** E24
Lilliput Ct BT15
off Clanmorris St **14** N12
Lime Ct BT13 **20** L14
Limegrove BT15 **9** M5
Limehill Gro BT14
off Leginn St **13** F9
Limehill St BT14 **12** E9
Limepark Ms BT14
off Lavens Dr **13** F10
Limepark St BT14
off Lavens Dr **13** F10
Limestone Rd BT15 **14** L11
Limewood Gro BT4
off Kincora Av **22** W15
Lincoln Av BT14 **20** L13
Lincoln Pl BT12 **30** C4
Lincoln Sq BT12
off Abyssinia St **19** K16
Linden Gdns BT14 **14** K11
Lindsay Ct BT7
off Lindsay St **31** E5
Lindsay St BT7 **30** D5
Lindsay Way BT7 **31** E5
Linen Ct BT5 **21** T17
Linen Gdns BT5 **21** T17
Linen Gro BT14 **13** F9
Linen Hall St BT2 **30** D3
Linen Hall St W BT2 **30** D4
Linfield Av BT12
off Linfield Rd **30** B5
Linfield Dr BT12
off Linfield Rd **30** B4
Linfield Gdns BT12
off Linfield Rd **30** B5
Linfield Rd BT12 **30** B5
Linfield St BT12
off Linfield Rd **30** B5
Linview Ct BT12
off Excise Wk **19** K16
Lisavon Dr BT4 **21** T14
Lisavon Ms BT4 **21** T14
Lisavon Par BT4 **21** T14
Lisavon St BT4 **21** T14
Lisbon St BT5 **21** Q16
Lisbreen Pk BT15 **8** L8
Lisburn Av BT9 **25** J20
Lisburn Rd BT9 **25** H22
Lisdarragh Pk BT14 **8** K8
Lisfaddan Cres BT12 **30** A2
Lisfaddan Dr BT12 **30** A2
Lisfaddan Pl BT12 **30** A2
Lisfaddan Way BT12 **30** A2
Lislea Av BT9
off Lisburn Rd **25** H21
Lislea Dr BT9 **25** H21
Lisleen Rd BT5 **29** Z21
Lismain St BT6 **21** R18
Lismore St BT6 **21** Q17
Lismoyne Pk BT15 **8** L7
Lisnasharragh Pk BT6 **28** U21
Lisnasharragh Ter BT6
off Lisnasharragh Pk **28** U21
Lissan Cl BT6 **27** R21
Lissan Link BT6
off Lissan Cl **27** R21
Lisvarna Hts BT12 **19** K16
Lisvarna Pl BT12 **19** K16
Little Charlotte St BT7 **31** E6
Little Donegall St BT1 **20** M14
Little Georges St BT15
off Henry St **20** M13
Little Grosvenor St BT12
off Burnaby Pl **19** K16
Little May St BT2 **31** E3
Little Patrick St BT15 **20** N14
Little Victoria St BT2 **30** C4
Little York St BT15 **20** N14
Locan St BT12 **19** H16
Lochinver Dr BT5 **23** AA18
Lockside Ct BT9 **26** M21
Locksley Dr BT10 **25** F23
Locksley Gdns BT10 **25** F24
Locksley Gra BT10 **25** F23
Locksley Par BT10 **25** F24
Locksley Pk BT10 **25** F23
Locksley Pl BT10
off Locksley Pk **25** F23
Lockview Rd BT9 **26** M21
Lombard St BT1 **30** D1
Lomond Av BT4 **21** T15
Lomond St BT4 **21** T15
London Rd BT6 **21** Q18
London St BT6 **21** Q17
Longacre BT8 **27** P23
Loopland Cres BT6 **21** R18
Loopland Dr BT6 **21** R18
Loopland Gdns BT6 **21** S18
Loopland Gro BT6 **21** S18
Loopland Par BT6
off Loopland Pk **21** S18
Loopland Pk BT6 **21** S18
Loopland Rd BT6 **21** S18
Lord St BT5 **21** R16
Lord St Ms BT5
off Lord St **21** R17
Lorne St BT9 **26** K19
Lothair Av BT15 **14** L11
Lothian Av BT5 **23** AA18
Louden St BT13 **30** A1
Lough Lea BT5 **21** Q15
Loughrey Ct BT15 **14** L10
Loughview BT14 **13** G8
Loughview Av, Hol. BT18 **11** Z8
Loughview Cl BT14 **13** G8
Loughview Dr BT6 **27** R23
Loughview Glen BT14 **13** G8
Loughview Grn BT14 **13** G8
Loughview Hts BT14 **13** G8
Loughview Manor BT14 **13** G8
Loughview Meadows BT14 **13** G8
Loughview St BT14
off Crumlin Rd **13** F10
Loughview Ter BT15 **14** N10
Louisa Ct BT14 **14** K12
Lovatt St BT5
off Ravenscroft Av **21** T16
Lower Braniel Rd BT5 **28** W20
Lower Clara Cres BT5
off Clara Av **21** T17
Lower Clonard St BT12 **19** J16
Lower Ctyd BT7 **26** N21
Lower Cres BT7 **20** M18
Lower Garfield St BT1 **30** D1
Lower Kilburn St BT12 **19** J17
Lower Mt St BT5
off Mount St **21** Q16
Lower Regent St BT13 **20** M14
Lower Rockview St BT12 **19** J17
Lower Stanfield St BT7 **31** F4
Lower Windsor Av BT9 **25** J19
Lowland Av BT5 **23** AA18
Lowland Gdns BT5
off Lowland Av **23** AA18
Lowland Wk BT5
off Kilmory Gdns **23** AA18
Lowry Ct BT6 **27** P23
Lowwood Gdns BT15 **9** N7
Lowwood Pk BT15 **9** M7
Lucerne Par BT9 **26** M21
Lucknow St BT13
off Cupar St **19** H15
Ludlow Sq BT15 **20** M13
Lupus Gro BT14 **13** F9
Luxembourg Ct BT15 **14** L9
Luxor Gdns BT5 **21** T17
Lyle Ct BT13
off Agnes St **19** K13
Lyndhurst Av BT13 **18** E13
Lyndhurst Cl BT13 **18** F13
Lyndhurst Ct BT13 **18** E13
Lyndhurst Cres BT13 **18** E13
Lyndhurst Dr BT13 **18** F13
Lyndhurst Gdns BT13 **18** F13
Lyndhurst Gro BT13 **18** F13
Lyndhurst Hts BT13 **18** E13
Lyndhurst Link BT13 **18** F13
Lyndhurst Meadows BT13 **18** E13
Lyndhurst Par BT13 **18** F13
Lyndhurst Pk BT13 **18** F13
Lyndhurst Path BT13 **18** E13
Lyndhurst Pl BT13 **18** E13
Lyndhurst Ri BT13 **18** F13
Lyndhurst Row BT13 **18** E13
Lyndhurst Vw BT13 **18** E13
Lyndhurst Vw Av BT13 **18** E13
Lyndhurst Vw Cl BT13 **18** E13
Lyndhurst Vw Pk BT13 **18** E13
Lyndhurst Vw Rd BT13 **18** E13
Lyndhurst Wk BT13 **18** E13
Lyndhurst Way BT13 **18** F13
Lynwood Pk, Hol. BT18 **11** AA7

M

Mabel Ct BT12 **30** A6
Mabel St BT12
off Utility St **30** A6
McAdam Gdns BT12
off Linfield Rd **30** B5
McAdam Pk BT12 **30** B5
McAllister Ct BT4
off Mersey St **21** S15
McAllister Ms BT4
off Mersey St **21** S15
McArthur Ct BT4 **21** R15
Macart Rd BT3 **20** P14
McAuley St BT7 **31** F5
McCandless St BT13 **19** J13
McCaughan Pk BT6 **28** T21
McCaughey Rd BT3 **15** Q12
McCavanas Pl BT2 **30** D4
McCleery St BT15
off North Hill St **20** M13
McClintock St BT2 **30** C4
McClure St BT7 **20** M18
McDonnell Ct BT12
off Servia St **19** K16
McDonnell St BT12 **19** K16
McIvor's Pl BT13
off Brown St **30** C1
Mackey St BT15 **14** M12
McKibben's Ct BT1
off North St **20** M14
McMaster St BT5 **21** R15
McMullans La BT6 **21** Q17
McQuillan St BT13
off Colligan St **19** J16
Madison Av BT15 **14** L10
Madison Av E BT4 **21** T15
Madras St BT13 **19** J13
Madrid Ct BT5
off Madrid St **21** Q16
Madrid St BT5 **21** Q16
Magdala St BT7 **20** M18
Maghies Pl BT6
off Pearl St **21** R17
Majestic Dr BT12 **30** B6
Major St BT5 **21** R15
Malcolmson St BT13 **19** J16
Maldon Ct BT12 **19** J17
Maldon St BT12 **19** J17
Malfin Dr BT9 **25** G24
Malinmore Pk BT11 **24** B22
Malone Av BT9 **26** K19
Malone Beeches BT9
off Norton Dr **25** J23
Malone Chase BT9 **26** L20
Malone Ct BT9 **25** J23
Malone Ct Ms BT9
off Malone Ct **25** J23
Malone Gra BT9 **26** K23
Malone Hill Pk BT9 **25** J23
Malone Meadows BT9 **25** J24
Malone Pk BT9 **25** H22
Malone Pk Cen BT9 **25** J23
Malone Pk La BT9 **25** H22
Malone Pl BT12 **20** L18
Malton Dr BT9 **25** G24
Malton Fold BT9 **25** G24
Malvern Cl BT13 **19** K13
Malvern Pl BT13
off Malvern St **20** L14
Malvern St BT13 **20** L14
Malvern Way BT13 **20** L14
Malwood Cl BT9
off Finwood Pk **25** G24
Manderson St BT4 **21** S15
Manna Gro BT5 **21** T18
Mann's Rd BT5 **29** AA21
Manor, The BT10 **24** C24
Manor Cl BT14 **14** L12
Manor Ct BT14 **14** K12
Manor Dr BT14 **14** K12
Manor Ms BT10 **24** C24
Manor St BT14 **14** K12
Mansfield St BT13
off Downing St **19** K14
Maple Ct, Hol. BT18
off Loughview Av **11** Z8
Mara Gdns, Hol. BT18
off Strand Av **11** Z5
Maralin Pl BT15
off Sheridan St **20** M13
Marchioness Grn BT12
off Marchioness St **19** K16
Marchioness St BT12 **19** K16
March St BT13 **19** H14
Marcus Ward St BT7 **30** D5
Marfield St BT4
off St. Leonards St **21** R15
Marguerite Pk BT10 **25** F23
Marina Pk BT5 **28** U19
Marine Par, Hol. BT18 **11** Z5
Marino Pk, Hol. BT18 **11** BB4
Market St BT1 **31** F3
Market St BT7 **31** F4

Marlborough Av BT9		
off Lisburn Av	25	J20
Marlborough Ct BT1		
off Queens Sq	31	F1
Marlborough Ct BT9		
off Lisburn Rd	25	J20
Marlborough Gdns BT9	26	K21
Marlborough Gate BT9	26	K21
Marlborough Hts BT6	28	U21
Marlborough Pk BT9	26	K21
Marlborough Pk Cen BT9	25	J21
Marlborough Pk Cross Av BT9	26	K21
Marlborough Pk N BT9	25	J20
Marlborough Pk S BT9	25	J21
Marlborough St BT1	31	F1
Marlfield Dr BT5	29	X19
Marlfield Ri BT5	29	Y19
Marmont Cres BT4	16	W12
Marmont Dr BT4	16	W12
Marmont Pk BT4	16	W12
Marmount Gdns BT14	13	H10
Marquis St BT1	30	C2
Marsden Gdns BT15	14	L10
Marsden Gdns Flats BT15		
off Marsden Gdns	14	L10
Marsden Ter BT15		
off Marsden Gdns	14	L10
Marshalls Rd BT5	28	T19
Marshall St BT1		
off Dunbar St	30	N14
Martello Ter, Hol. BT18	11	AA6
Martinez Av BT5	21	T16
Martin St BT5	21	R16
Marylebone Pk BT9	26	M22
Maryville Av BT9	25	J20
Maryville Ct BT7		
off Maryville St	30	D5
Maryville Pk BT9	25	H21
Maryville St BT7	30	D6
Mashona Ct BT6	21	R18
Massareene Path BT12		
off Cullingtree Rd	19	K16
Massey Av BT4	23	Y14
Massey Ct BT4	23	Z14
Massey Grn BT4	23	Y14
Massey Pk BT4	23	Z14
Matchett St BT13	19	J13
Matilda Av BT12	30	B6
Matilda Dr BT12	30	B6
Matilda Gdns BT12	30	A6
Mawhinneys Ct BT13		
off Melbourne St	30	B1
Maxwells Pl BT12		
off Maxwell St	30	B6
Maxwell St BT12	30	B6
Mayfair Av BT6	27	S20
Mayfair Ct BT14		
off Ardilea St	14	K12
Mayfield Cl BT10	24	C23
Mayfield Sq BT10	24	C23
Mayfield St BT9	25	J20
Mayflower St BT5	21	S17
Maymount St BT6	21	Q17
Mayo Ct BT13	19	H14
Mayo Link BT13		
off Mayo St	19	H14
Mayo Pk BT13	19	H14
Mayo Pl BT13	19	H14
Mayo St BT13	19	H14
Mays Meadow BT1	31	G3
May St BT1	31	E3
Meadowbank Pl BT9	25	J19
Meadowbank St BT9	26	K19
Meadow Cl BT15	14	M12
Meadow Pl BT15	14	M12
Medway Ct BT4		
off Medway St	21	R15
Medway St BT4	21	R15
Meekon St BT4	21	S15
Melbourne Ct BT1		
off Melbourne St	30	B1
Melbourne St BT13	30	B2
Melfort Dr BT5	23	Z24
Melrose Av BT5	21	T16
Melrose St BT9	26	K19
Mendi St BT12	19	J17
Merkland Pl BT13	19	H15
Merkland St BT13	19	H15
Merok Cres BT6	28	T20
Merok Dr BT6	28	T20
Merok Gdns BT6	28	T21
Merok Pk BT6	28	T21
Merryfield Dr BT15	8	K8
Mersey St BT4	21	S15
Merston Gdns, New. BT36	9	M4
Mervue Ct BT15	14	M12
Mervue St BT15	14	M12
Meyrick Pk BT14	8	H8
Mica Dr BT12	19	G16
Mica St BT12	19	H16
Middle Braniel Rd BT5	29	X22
Middlepath St BT5	31	G1
Midland Cl BT15	14	N12
Midland Cres BT15		
off Midland Cl	14	N12
Midland Ter BT15	14	N12
Mileriver St BT15	14	M11
Milewater Rd BT3	15	P11
Milewater St BT15	14	N12
Milford Pl BT12	30	A2
Milford Ri BT12	30	A2
Milford St BT12	30	A2
Milk St BT5		
off Bloomfield Av	21	T16
Millar St BT6	21	Q18
Mill Av BT14	12	E8
Millbank Pk BT14		
off Wolfend Dr	13	F9
Millennium Way BT12	19	G16
Millfield BT1	30	C1
Mill Pond Ct BT5	21	S16
Mill St W BT13	19	J13
Milltown Row BT12	19	G18
Mill Valley Av BT14	12	E9
Mill Valley Ct BT14	12	E10
Mill Valley Cres BT14	12	E10
Mill Valley Dr BT14	12	E10
Mill Valley La BT14	12	E10
Mill Valley N BT14	12	E10
Mill Valley Pl BT14	12	E10
Mill Valley Rd BT14	12	E10
Millview Ct BT14	13	F9
Milner St BT12	19	J17
Minds Way BT9	20	L18
Mineral St BT15	14	N10
Mizen Gdns BT11	24	B21
Moffatt St BT15	20	M13
Moira Ct BT5	21	Q16
Moltke St BT12	19	J18
Molyneaux St BT15		
off Henry St	20	N13
Monagh Cres BT11	18	D18
Monagh Dr BT11	18	D17
Monagh Gro BT11	18	D17
Monagh Link BT11	18	D18
Monagh Par BT11	18	D17
Monagh Rd BT11	18	D18
Monagh Rd Bypass BT11	18	D18
Monarch Par BT12	19	J17
Monarch St BT12	19	J17
Moneyrea St BT6	21	R17
Montgomery Ct BT6	27	S20
Montgomery Rd BT6	27	S20
Montgomery St BT1	31	E2
Montreal St BT13	19	H13
Montrose St BT5	21	R15
Montrose St S BT5	21	R16
Montrose Wk BT5		
off Montrose St	21	R15
Moonstone St BT9	25	J21
Mooreland Cres BT11	25	F21
Mooreland Dr BT11	24	E21
Mooreland Pk BT11	24	E21
Moores Pl BT13	30	B6
Moorfield St BT5	21	T16
Moorgate St BT5	21	T16
Moor Pk Av BT10	24	C23
Moor Pk Dr BT10	24	C23
Moor Pk Gdns BT10	24	C23
Moor Pk Ms BT10	24	C23
Mornington BT7	26	N22
Mornington Ms BT7		
off Mornington	26	N22
Mornington Pk BT7	26	N22
Mornington Pl BT7	26	N22
Morpeth St BT13		
off Tyne St	19	K14
Moscow Rd BT3	16	U10
Moscow St BT13		
off Shankill Rd	19	K14
Moss Rd, Hol. BT18	17	AA12
Mossvale St BT13	19	H13
Motelands BT4	17	X12
Mount, The BT5	21	Q16
Mount Aboo Pk BT10	24	E24
Mountainhill La BT14		
off Mountainhill Rd	12	E9
Mountainhill Rd BT14	12	E9
Mountainhill Wk BT14		
off Mountainhill Rd	12	E9
Mountainview Dr BT14	13	G12
Mountainview Gdns BT14	13	G12
Mountainview Par BT14	13	G12
Mountainview Pk BT14	13	G12
Mountainview Pl BT14	13	G12
Mount Alverno BT12	18	D17
Mount Charles BT7	20	M18
Mount Coole Gdns BT14	8	J8
Mount Coole Pk BT14	8	J8
Mount Eden Ct BT13	13	H12
Mount Eden Pk BT9	25	J23
Mountforde Ct BT5		
off Mountforde	21	Q15
Mountforde Dr BT5	21	Q15
Mountforde Gdns BT5		
off Mountforde Dr	21	Q15
Mountforde Pk BT5		
off Mountforde Rd	21	Q15
Mountforde Rd BT5	21	Q15
Mountjoy St BT13	19	J14
Mount Merrion BT6	27	R20
Mount Merrion Av BT6	27	R21
Mount Merrion Cres BT6	27	Q21
Mount Merrion Dr BT6	27	R21
Mount Merrion Gdns BT6	27	R21
Mount Merrion Pk BT6	27	Q22
Mount Michael Dr BT8	27	R24
Mount Michael Gro BT8	27	R24
Mount Michael Pk BT8	27	R24
Mount Michael Vw BT8	27	R24
Mount Oriel BT8	27	Q24
Mount Pleasant BT9	26	M20
Mountpottinger Link BT5	21	Q15
Mountpottinger Rd BT5	21	Q16
Mount Prospect Pk BT9	19	K18
Mount St BT5	21	Q16
Mount St BT6	21	Q16
Mount St, New. BT36	9	N4
Mount St S BT6	21	Q17
Mount Vernon Ct BT15		
off Mount Vernon La	9	N8
Mount Vernon Dr BT15	9	N8
Mount Vernon Gdns BT15	9	M8
Mount Vernon Gro BT15		
off Mount Vernon Pk	9	N8
Mount Vernon La BT15	9	N8
Mount Vernon Ms BT15	9	M8
Mount Vernon Pas BT15	9	N8
Mount Vernon Rd BT15	9	N8
Mount Vernon Wk BT15	9	N8
Mountview Ct BT14	14	K12
Mountview St BT14	14	K12
Mourne Par BT5		
off Hornby St	21	R15
Mourne St BT5	21	S16
Mowhan St BT9	25	J21
Moyallon Gdns BT7	27	P22
Moyard Cres BT12	18	E15
Moyard Par BT12	18	E16
Moyard Pk BT12	18	E15
Moyne Pk BT5	29	Z19
Mulhouse Rd BT12	19	K16
Murray St BT1	30	C3
Musgrave Channel Rd BT3	21	R13
Musgrave Pk Ct BT9		
off Stockmans La	25	G22
Musgrave St BT1		
off Ann St	31	F2
Music Hall Ct BT1		
off Music Hall La	31	E3
Music Hall La BT1	31	E3
My Ladys Mile, Hol. BT18	11	Z6
My Ladys Rd BT6	21	Q17
Myrtlefield Pk BT9	25	H22

N

Nansen St BT12	19	H17
Napier St BT12		
off Blondin St	20	L18
Naroon Pk BT11	24	B20
Nassau St BT13		
off Beresford St	19	K14
Navan Grn BT11	24	D20
Navarra Pl, New. BT36	9	M4
Neills Hill Pk BT5	22	V17
Nelson Ct BT13	19	J14
Nelson Sq BT13		
off Nelson Ct	19	J14
Nelson St BT15	20	N14
Nendrum Gdns BT5	21	T17
Netherleigh Pk BT4	23	Y14
Nevis Av BT4	21	T15
New Barnsley Cres BT12	18	D16
New Barnsley Dr BT12	18	E16
New Barnsley Gdns BT12	18	E15
New Barnsley Grn BT12	18	E16
New Barnsley Gro BT12	18	E16
New Barnsley Par BT12	18	E16
New Barnsley Pk BT12	18	E16
Newcastle Manor BT4	21	R15
Newcastle St BT4	21	R15
New Fm La BT14		
off Leginn St	13	F9
Newforge Dale BT9	26	K23
New Forge Gra BT9	26	K23
Newforge La BT9	26	K23
Newington Av BT15	14	L11
Newington St BT15	14	M11
New Lo Gdns BT15	20	M13
New Lo Pl BT15		
off New Lo Rd	20	M13
New Lo Rd BT15	14	M12
Newport Ct BT14	14	K12
Newry St BT6	21	R17
Newton Gdns, New. BT36	9	N4
Newton Pk BT8	27	Q24
Newtownards Rd BT4	21	Q15
Ninth St BT13	19	K14
Norbloom Gdns BT15	21	T17
Norbury St BT11	18	F18
Norfolk Dr BT11	18	F18
Norfolk Gdns BT11	18	E18
Norfolk Gro BT11	18	E18
Norfolk Par BT11	18	E18
Norfolk Rd BT11	18	E18
Norfolk Way BT11	18	E18
Norglen Ct BT11	18	E17
Norglen Cres BT11	18	E17
Norglen Dr BT11	18	E18
Norglen Gdns BT11	18	D18
Norglen Gro BT11	18	E18
Norglen Par BT11	18	D17
Norglen Rd BT11	18	D18
North Bk BT6	27	R20
North Boundary St BT13	20	L14

Name	No	Ref
Northbrook Gdns BT9	25	J19
Northbrook St BT9	25	J19
North Circular Rd BT14	8	K8
North Circular Rd BT15	8	K7
North Cl, Hol. BT18	11	Z7
North Derby St BT15	14	N11
Northern Ireland Science		
Pk BT3	15	R12
Northern Rd BT3	15	P11
Northfield Ri BT5	28	W19
North Gdns BT5	22	U17
North Grn BT11	24	D20
North Hill St BT15	20	M13
North Howard Ct BT13		
off Fifth St	19	K15
North Howard Link		
BT13	19	K15
North Howard St BT13	19	K15
North Howard Wk		
BT13	19	K14
North King St BT13		
off Gardiner St	20	L14
Northland Ct BT13		
off Northland St	19	J14
Northlands Pk BT10	24	D23
Northland St BT13	19	J14
North Link BT11	24	E20
North Par BT7	27	P20
North Queen St BT15	20	M13
North Rd BT4	22	U15
North Rd BT5	22	U17
North Sperrin BT5	23	AA17
North St BT1	20	M14
North St Arc BT1		
off North St	20	M15
Northumberland St		
BT13	19	K15
Northwick Dr BT14	13	H11
Northwood Cres BT15	14	N10
Northwood Dr BT15	14	N10
Northwood Par BT15	14	N10
Northwood Rd BT15	14	N10
Norton Dr BT9	25	J23
Norwood Av BT4	22	V15
Norwood Ct BT4	22	V14
Norwood Cres BT4	22	V14
Norwood Dr BT4	22	V15
Norwood Gdns BT4	22	W14
Norwood Gro BT4	22	V14
Norwood La, Hol. BT18	11	Z7
Norwood Pk BT4	22	W14
Norwood St BT12		
off Wellwood St	30	C5
Notting Hill BT9	26	K21
Notting Hill Ct BT9	26	L21
Notting Hill Manor BT9	26	K21
Nubia St BT12	19	J18
Nun's Wk, Hol. BT18	11	AA8

O

Name	No	Ref
Oakdale St BT5	21	S16
Oakdene Dr BT4	21	T14
Oakdene Par BT4	21	T14
Oakfield St BT14	13	J12
Oakhill BT5	28	V21
Oakhurst Av BT10	24	C24
Oakland Av BT4	22	U16
Oakleigh Pk BT6	21	Q18
Oakley Av, Hol. BT18	11	Z8
Oakley St BT14	13	F10
Oakman St BT12	19	H16
Oakmount Dr BT15	14	N9
Oak St BT7		
off Elm St	30	D6
Oak Way BT7	30	D6
Oakwood Ct BT9	25	J23
Oakwood Gro BT9	25	J23
Oakwood Ms BT9	25	J23
Oakwood Pk BT9	25	J23
Oban St BT12	20	L18
Oberon St BT6	27	R19
Oceanic Av BT15	14	L11
O'Dempsey St BT15	14	N10
Odessa St BT13	19	J15
Ogilvie St BT6	21	R18
Ohio St BT13	19	H13
Old Bakers Ct BT6	21	Q18
Old Brewery La BT11	24	D19
Old Cavehill Rd BT15	8	K7
Old Channel Rd BT3	20	P14
Old Dundonald Rd		
(Dundonald) BT16	23	BB17
Old Golf Course Rd		
(Dunmurry) BT17	24	B24
Old Holywood Rd BT4	22	X13
Old Holywood Rd, Hol.		
BT18	17	Z9
Old Mill Rd BT14	12	E9
Old Mill Way BT14		
off Old Mill Rd	13	F9
Oldpark Av BT14	14	K11
Oldpark Rd BT14	13	H9
Oldpark Sq BT14		
off Ardoyne Av	13	J12
Oldpark Ter BT14	13	J10
Old Quay Ct, Hol. BT18	11	BB5
Old Quay Rd, Hol.		
BT18	11	BB4
Old Westland Rd BT14	14	K9
Olive St BT13	19	H13
Olympia Dr BT12	25	J19
Olympia Par BT12	25	J19
Olympia St BT12	25	J19
Omeath St BT6	21	R18
O'Neills Pl, Hol. BT18	11	AA6
O'Neill St BT13	19	J16
Onslow Gdns BT6	27	R20
Onslow Par BT6	27	R20
Onslow Pk BT6	27	R20
Ophir Gdns BT15	8	K8
Orangefield Av BT5	22	U17
Orangefield Cres BT5	27	S19
Orangefield Dr BT5	22	U17
Orangefield Dr S BT5	22	U17
Orangefield Gdns BT5	22	U17
Orangefield Grn BT5	22	U17
Orangefield Gro BT5	22	U17
Orangefield La BT5	22	U17
Orangefield Par BT5	22	U17
Orangefield Pk BT5	22	U18
Orangefield Rd BT5	22	U17
Oranmore Dr BT11	24	B23
Oranmore St BT13	19	J15
Orby Chase BT5	21	T17
Orby Ct BT5	21	T18
Orby Dr BT5	21	T18
Orby Gdns BT5	21	S18
Orby Gra BT5	21	T18
Orby Grn BT5	21	S18
Orby Gro BT5	21	T18
Orby Link BT5	21	S18
Orby Ms BT5	21	T18
Orby Mills BT5	21	S18
Orby Par BT5	21	T18
Orby Pk BT5	21	T18
Orby Pl BT5	28	T19
Orby Rd BT5	21	S18
Orby St BT5	28	U19
Orchard Cl BT5	23	Y18
Orchard Ct, Hol. BT18	17	X11
Orchard La BT4	22	W14
Orchard St BT15	14	N12
Orchardvale BT6	28	T21
Orchardville Av BT10	24	E23
Orchardville Cres BT10	24	E23
Orchardville Gdns		
BT10	24	E23
Oregon Gdns BT13	19	J13
Orient Gdns BT14	14	L11
Orkney St BT13	19	J14
Ormeau Av BT2	30	D5
Ormeau Br BT7	26	N19
Ormeau Embk BT6	31	G6
Ormeau Embk BT7	27	P19
Ormeau Rd BT7	31	E6
Ormeau St BT7	31	E6
Ormiston Cres BT4	22	W16
Ormiston Dr BT4	22	X16
Ormiston Gdns BT5	22	W16
Ormiston Par BT4	22	X16
Ormiston Pk BT4	22	X16
Ormiston Sq BT4	22	W15
Ormonde Av BT10	24	E24
Ormonde Cres BT6	21	S18
Ormonde Gdns BT6	21	S18
Ormonde Pk BT10	24	D24
Ormond Pl BT12		
off Roumania Ri	19	K15
Orpen Av BT10	24	E24
Orpen Dr BT10	24	E24
Orpen Pk BT10	24	E24
Orpen Rd BT10	24	E24
Osborne Dr BT9	25	J21
Osborne Gdns BT9	25	J22
Osborne Pk BT9	25	H21
Osborne Pl BT9	25	H21
Osman St BT12	19	K16
Oswald Pk BT12	30	A6
Ottawa St BT13	19	H13
Oval Ct BT4		
off Oval St	21	S15
Oval St BT4	21	S15
Owenvale Ms BT13	18	F15
Owenvarragh Gdns BT11		
off Owenvarragh Pk	25	F21
Owenvarragh Pk BT11	24	E21
Oxford St BT1	31	F2

P

Name	No	Ref
Pacific Av BT15	14	L11
Pakenham Ms BT7		
off Pakenham St	30	D6
Pakenham St BT7	30	C6
Palace Gdns BT15	14	L9
Palace Gro, Hol. BT18	17	Z9
Palestine St BT7	26	N19
Palmer Ct BT13		
off Palmer St	13	H12
Palmerston Pk BT4	22	U13
Palmerston Rd BT4	22	U14
Palmer St BT13	19	H13
Pandora St BT12	19	K18
Pansy St BT4	21	S15
Panton St BT12		
off Ross Rd	19	K15
Paris St BT13	19	K14
Park Av BT4	21	T14
Park Av, Hol. BT18	11	AA6
Park Cen BT12	19	H17
Park Dr, Hol. BT18	11	Z6
Parkend St BT15	14	M11
Parker St BT5	21	R15
Parkgate Av BT4	21	T15
Parkgate Cres BT4	21	S15
Parkgate Dr BT4	21	S15
Parkgate Gdns BT4	21	T15
Parkgate Par BT4	21	T15
Park Gra BT4		
off Park Av	21	T15
Park La BT9	26	L19
Parkmore Ct BT7	27	P20
Parkmount Cl BT15	14	N11
Parkmount Gdns BT15	9	N6
Parkmount La BT15	9	N6
Parkmount Pl BT15	9	N6
Parkmount Rd BT15	9	M7
Parkmount St BT15	14	N11
Parkmount Pas BT15	9	N6
Parkmount Ter BT15	9	N6
Parkmount Way BT15	9	N6
Park Par BT6	21	Q17
Park Pl BT6	21	Q18
Park Rd BT7	27	P20
Park Royal Balmoral BT9		
off Lisburn Rd	25	G22
Parkside Gdns BT15	14	M11
Parkview Ct BT14		
off Glenview St	14	K12
Parkville St BT15	14	L9
Parkvue Manor BT5	23	Y18
Pasadena Gdns BT5	22	W16
Patterson's Pl BT1		
off Upper Arthur St	31	E3
Pattons La, Hol. BT18		
off Church Vw	11	Z6
Paulett Av BT5		
off Albertbridge Rd	21	R16
Pavilions Office Pk, Hol.		
BT18	11	Y6
Paxton St BT5	21	R16
Pearl Ct BT6	21	R17
Pearl St BT6	21	R17
Pembridge Ct BT4	22	W15
Pembridge Ms BT5	22	V17
Pembroke St BT12	19	K18
Penge Gdns BT9	26	M21
Penrose St BT7	20	N18
Pepperhill St BT13		
off Stanhope Dr	20	M14
Percy Pl BT13	20	L14
Percy St BT13	19	K15
Pernau St BT13	19	K14
Perry Ct BT5	21	Q16
Peters Hill BT13	20	L14
Phennick Dr BT10	25	F24
Picardy Av BT6	27	S20
Pilot Pl BT1		
off Pilot St	20	P13
Pilot St BT1	20	P13
Pims Av BT4	21	T15
Pim St BT15	20	M13
Pine Crest, Hol. BT18	11	AA7
Pine Gro, Hol. BT18		
off Loughview Av	11	Z8
Pine St BT7	31	E6
Pine Way BT7	31	E6
Piney Hills BT9	26	K24
Piney La BT9	26	K24
Piney Pk BT9	26	K24
Piney Wk BT9	26	K24
Piney Way BT9	26	K24
Pinkerton Wk BT15	20	M13
Pirrie Pk Gdns BT6	27	Q19
Pirrie Rd BT4	22	W15
Pitt Pl BT4	21	Q15
Pittsburg St BT15	14	N10
Plas Merdyn, Hol. BT18	11	BB7
Plateau, The BT9	26	K24
Plevna Pk BT12		
off Osman St	19	K16
Plunkett Ct BT13		
off Plunkett St	20	M14
Plunkett St BT13	20	M14
Pollard Cl BT12	19	H15
Pollard St BT12	19	H15
Pollock Rd BT3	15	P12
Pommern Par BT6	27	S19
Pomona Av BT4	21	T15
Ponsonby Av BT15	14	L12
Portallo St BT6	21	R18
Porter Pk BT10	24	E24
Portland Pl BT15	20	M14
Portnamona Ct BT11	24	D19
Posnett Ct BT7	30	D6
Posnett St BT7	30	C6
Pottingers Ct BT1		
off Ann St	31	E2
Pottingers Entry BT1		
off High St	31	E2
Pottinger St BT5	21	R17
Powerscourt Pl BT7	20	N18
Premier Dr BT15	14	M9
Premier Gro BT15	14	M10
Prestwick Dr BT14	13	H9
Prestwick Pk BT14	13	H9
Pretoria St BT9	26	M19
Primrose St BT7	27	P20
Primrose St BT14	13	F10
Prince Andrew Gdns		
BT12	19	K17
Prince Andrew Pk		
BT12	19	K17
Prince Edward Dr BT9	26	M22
Prince Edward Gdns		
BT9	26	M22
Prince Edward Pk BT9	26	M21
Prince of Wales Av BT4	23	Z16
Prince Regent Rd BT5	28	V20
Princes Ct BT1		
off Queens Sq	31	F1
Princes Dock St BT1	20	P13
Princes St BT1		
off Queens Sq	31	F1
Princes St Ct BT1		
off Queens Sq	31	F1
Prior's Lea, Hol. BT18		
off Firmount Cres	17	Z9
Priory End, Hol. BT18	11	Z7
Priory Gdns BT10	25	F23
Priory Pk BT10	25	F23

Name	Page	Grid
Priory Pk, Hol. BT18	11	AA5
Prospect Pk BT14	13	J12
Prospect Ter, Hol. BT18		
off Kinnegar Rd	11	Y6
Purdys La BT8	27	Q24
Q		
Quadrant Pl BT12	30	A2
Quarry Hill BT5	28	W21
Quarry Rd BT4	17	X12
Queen Elizabeth Br BT1	31	F1
Queen Elizabeth Br BT3	31	F1
Queens Arc BT1	30	D2
Queensberry Pk BT6	27	Q22
Queen's Br BT1	31	F2
Queen's Br BT4	31	G1
Queensland St BT13	19	K13
Queens Par BT15	20	M13
Queens Quay BT3	31	G1
Queens Quay Rd BT3	20	P14
Queens Rd BT3	20	P14
Queens Sq BT1	31	F1
Queen St BT1	30	C3
Queen Victoria Gdns BT15	14	M10
Queen Victoria St BT5	21	T16
Quinton St BT5	21	S17
Quinville, Hol. BT18		
off Spencer St	11	AA6
R		
Raby St BT7	27	P20
Radnor St BT6	21	Q17
Rainey Way BT7		
off Lindsay St	30	D5
Raleigh St BT13	19	K13
Ramoan Dr BT11	24	C20
Ramoan Gdns BT11	24	C20
Randal Pk BT9	25	J21
Ranelagh St BT6	21	R18
Ranfurly Dr BT4	22	U15
Raphael St BT7	31	E5
Ratcliffe St BT7	30	C6
Rathbone St BT2		
off Little May St	31	E3
Rathcool St BT9	25	J20
Rathdrum St BT9	25	J20
Rathgar St BT9	25	J20
Rathlin St BT13	19	H13
Rath Mor BT11	24	C22
Rathmore St BT6	21	Q17
Ravenhill Av BT6	21	Q18
Ravenhill Ct BT6	21	Q18
Ravenhill Cres BT6	21	Q18
Ravenhill Gdns BT6	27	Q19
Ravenhill Ms BT6	21	Q18
Ravenhill Par BT6	21	R18
Ravenhill Pk BT6	27	Q20
Ravenhill Pk Gdns BT6	27	Q20
Ravenhill Reach BT6	31	H5
Ravenhill Reach Ct BT6		
off Ravenhill Reach	31	H5
Ravenhill Reach Ms BT6	31	H5
Ravenhill Rd BT6	27	P21
Ravenhill St BT6	21	Q17
Ravenscroft Av BT5	21	T16
Ravenscroft St BT5	21	T16
Ravensdale Ct BT5	21	R17
Ravensdale Cres BT5	21	R17
Ravensdale St BT5	21	R17
Ravensdene Cres BT6	27	Q19
Ravensdene Ms BT6	27	Q19
Ravensdene Pk BT6	27	Q19
Ravensdene Pk Gdns BT6	27	Q20
Ravenswood Cres BT5	29	X20
Ravenswood Pk BT5	28	W20
Redburn Sq, Hol. BT18	11	Z6
Redcar St BT6	21	R18
Redcliffe Dr BT4	21	S15
Redcliffe Par BT4	21	S15
Redcliffe St BT4	21	S15
Regent St BT13	20	L13
Regent's Wd BT9	25	J24
Reid St BT6	27	R19
Renfrew Ho BT12		
off Rowland Way	30	B5
Renfrew Wk BT12		
off Rowland Way	30	B5
Renwick St BT12	30	C6
Riada Cl BT4	21	R15
Ribble St BT4	21	S15
Richardson Ct BT6		
off Richardson St	21	Q17
Richardson St BT6	21	Q17
Richdale Dr, Hol. BT18	11	BB4
Richhill Cres BT5	22	W17
Richhill Pk BT5	22	W18
Richmond Av, Hol. BT18	17	X10
Richmond Cl, Hol. BT18	17	X10
Richmond Ct, Hol. BT18	17	X10
Richmond Grn, Hol. BT18	17	X11
Richmond Hts, Hol. BT18	17	X10
Richmond Ms BT10	25	F23
Richmond Pk BT9	26	L22
Richmond Pk BT10	25	F23
Richmond Sq BT15	14	L10
Richview St BT12	19	K17
Ridgeway St BT9	26	M20
Riga St BT13	19	J14
Rigby Cl BT15	14	L9
Ringford Cres BT11	24	B22
Ringford Pk BT11		
off Ringford Cres	24	B22
Rinnalea Cl BT11	24	B21
Rinnalea Gdns BT11	24	B21
Rinnalea Gro BT11	24	B22
Rinnalea Wk BT11		
off Rinnalea Way	24	B21
Rinnalea Way BT11	24	B21
Ritchie St BT15	14	N11
River Cl BT11	24	C23
Riverdale Cl BT11	24	E21
Riverdale Gdns BT11	24	D21
Riverdale Pk Av BT11	24	D21
Riverdale Pk Dr BT11	24	D21
Riverdale Pk E BT11	24	E21
Riverdale Pk N BT11	24	D21
Riverdale Pk S BT11	24	D22
Riverdale Pk W BT11	24	D21
Riverdale Pl BT11	24	E21
Riversdale St BT13		
off North Boundary St	20	L14
Riverside Sq BT12		
off Roden Way	19	K16
Riverside Vw BT7	26	N22
Riverside Way BT12	19	K17
River Ter BT7	31	F6
Riverview St BT9	26	M20
Robina Ct BT15	14	M12
Robina St BT15	14	M11
Rochester Av BT6	27	S21
Rochester Ct BT6		
off Clonduff Dr	28	U20
Rochester Dr BT6	27	S21
Rochester Rd BT6	28	T21
Rochester St BT6	21	Q17
Rockdale St BT12	19	G17
Rock Gro BT12		
off Glenalina Cres	18	E17
Rockland St BT12	19	J17
Rockmore Rd BT12	19	G17
Rockmount St BT12	19	G17
Rockview St BT12	19	J18
Rockville Ct BT4	22	V13
Rockville Ms BT4	22	V13
Rockville St BT12	19	G17
Rocky Rd BT5	29	Z21
Rocky Rd BT6	27	S22
Rocky Rd BT8	28	T22
Roddens Cres BT5	28	V20
Roddens Gdns BT5	28	V20
Roddens Pk BT5	28	V20
Roden Pas BT12	19	K16
Roden Sq BT12		
off Roden Way	19	K16
Roden St BT12	19	K17
Roden Way BT12	19	K16
Rodney Dr BT12	19	H18
Rodney Par BT12	19	H18
Roosevelt Ri BT12	19	K17
Roosevelt Sq BT12	19	K17
Roosevelt St BT12	19	K17
Rosapenna Ct BT14		
off Rosapenna St	14	K12
Rosapenna Dr BT14	14	K12
Rosapenna Par BT14	14	K11
Rosapenna St BT14	14	K12
Rosapenna Wk BT14		
off Rosevale St	14	K12
Rosebank Ct BT14		
off Glenview St	14	K12
Rosebank St BT13		
off Ohio St	19	J13
Rosebery Gdns BT6	21	R18
Rosebery Rd BT6	21	Q17
Rosebery St BT5	21	T16
Roseland Pl BT12	30	A6
Roseleigh St BT14	14	K12
Rosemary Pk BT9	25	J24
Rosemary St BT1	30	D1
Rosemount Av BT5	23	AA16
Rosemount Gdns BT15	14	L10
Rosemount Pk BT5	28	V21
Rosepark BT5	23	AA16
Rosepark Cen BT5	23	AA16
Rosepark E BT5	23	AA16
Rosepark Meadows BT5		
off Rosepark	23	AA17
Rosepark S BT5	23	AA16
Rosepark W BT5	23	AA17
Rosetta Av BT7	27	P21
Rosetta Dr BT7	27	P22
Rosetta Par BT7	27	P22
Rosetta Pk BT6	27	Q21
Rosetta Rd BT6	27	Q21
Rosetta Rd E BT6	27	R22
Rosetta Way BT6	27	P21
Rosevale St BT14	14	K12
Rosewood Ct BT14	14	K12
Rosewood Pk BT6	28	V20
Rosewood St BT14	19	K13
Rosgoill Dr BT11	8	B21
Rosgoill Gdns BT11	24	B21
Rosgoill Pk BT11	24	C21
Roslin Gdns BT5	23	AA18
Roslyn St BT6	21	Q17
Rosscoole Pk BT14	8	J7
Ross Cotts BT12		
off Ross St	19	K15
Ross Ct BT12	19	K15
Ross Mill Av BT13	19	J15
Rossmore Av BT7	27	P21
Rossmore Dr BT7	27	P21
Rossmore Pk BT7	27	P21
Rossnareen Av BT11	24	C20
Rossnareen Ct BT11	24	C20
Rossnareen Pk BT11	24	C20
Rossnareen Rd BT11	24	C20
Ross Ri BT12		
off Ross Rd	19	K15
Ross Rd BT12	19	K15
Ross St BT12	19	K15
Rothsay St BT14		
off Ardilea St	13	J12
Rothsay St BT14		
off Glenpark St	13	J12
Rotterdam Ct BT5	31	G2
Rotterdam St BT5	31	G2
Roumania Ri BT12	19	K15
Roundhill St BT5	21	R16
Rowland Way BT12	30	B5
Royal Av BT1	30	D1
Rugby Av BT7	20	N18
Rugby Ct BT7	26	N19
Rugby Ms BT7		
off Rugby St	26	M19
Rugby Par BT7	26	M19
Rugby Rd BT7	20	M18
Rugby St BT7	26	M19
Rumford St BT13	19	K14
Runnymede Dr BT12	25	J19
Runnymede Par BT12	25	J19
Rushfield Av BT7	26	N21
Rusholme St BT13	19	K13
Russell Pk BT5	29	AA19
Russell Pl BT2	31	E4
Russell St BT2	31	E4
Rutherford St BT13		
off Hopewell Cres	20	L14
Rutherglen St BT13	13	G12
Rutland St BT7	20	N18
Rydalmere St BT12	19	J17
S		
Sackville Ct BT13	30	B1
Sagimor Gdns BT5	21	T16
St. Agnes Dr BT11	24	D21
St. Agnes Pl BT11	24	D21
St. Albans Gdns BT9	26	M20
St. Andrews Sq E BT12		
off Hope St	30	C4
St. Andrews Sq N BT12		
off Hope St	30	B4
St. Andrews Sq W BT12		
off Hope St	30	B4
St. Annes Cl BT10	24	D24
St. Annes Cres BT10	24	D24
St. Annes La BT10	24	D24
St. Aubyn St BT15	14	N10
St. Columbans Ct BT14		
off Glenview St	14	K12
Saintfield Rd BT8	27	P22
St. Gall's Av BT13	19	J15
St. Gemmas Ct BT14	13	J12
St. Georges Gdns BT12		
off Albion St	30	C6
St. Georges Harbour BT7	31	H4
St. George's Mkt BT1	31	F3
St. Gerards Manor BT12	18	D16
St. Helens Ct, Hol. BT18	11	Z6
St. Ives Gdns BT9	26	M20
St. James Av BT13		
off Highcairn Dr	18	F14
St. James Ms BT14	20	L13
St. James's Av BT12	19	H17
St. James's Cres BT12	19	G18
St. James's Dr BT12	19	G18
St. James's Gdns BT12	19	H17
St. James's Par BT12	19	G18
St. James's Pk BT12	19	H17
St. James's Pl BT12	19	G18
St. James's Rd BT12	19	G18
St. James's St BT12	20	L13
St. Johns Av BT7	27	P22
St. Johns Ct BT7		
off St. Johns Pk	27	P22
St. Johns Pk BT7	27	P22
St. John's Pl BT7	27	P22
St. John's Sq BT7	27	P22
St. Judes Av BT7	27	P21
St. Judes Cres BT7	27	P20
St. Judes Par BT7	27	P20
St. Judes Sq BT7	27	P20
St. Katharine Rd BT12	19	H18
St. Kilda Ct BT13	31	H5
St. Kilda St BT6	31	H5
St. Leonards Cres BT4		
off St. Leonards St	21	R15
St. Leonards St BT4	21	R15
St. Lukes Cl BT13		
off Carlow St	19	K14
St. Lukes Wk BT13		
off Carlow St	19	K15
St. Marys Ct BT13		
off Silvio St	19	K13
St. Marys Gdns BT12	19	G16
St. Matthew's Ct BT5		
off Seaforde St	21	Q15
St. Meryl Pk BT11	24	E19
St. Patrick's Wk BT4		
off Newtownards Rd	21	R15
St. Pauls Fold BT15		
off Canning St	14	N12
St. Pauls St BT15		
off Canning St	14	N12
St. Peters Cl BT12		
off Albert St	19	K15
St. Peters Ct BT12	19	K15
St. Peter's Pl BT12		
off Ardmoulin St	19	K15

Street	No.	Grid
St. Peters Sq E BT12		
off Ardmoulin St	19	K15
St. Peters Sq N BT12		
off Ardmoulin St	19	K15
St. Peters Sq S BT12		
off Ardmoulin St	19	K15
St. Stephens Ct BT13		
off Brown Sq	20	L14
St. Vincent St BT13	14	N10
Saleen Pk, Hol. BT18		
off Priory Pk	11	AA5
Salisbury Av BT15	8	L8
Salisbury Ct BT7	30	D6
Salisbury Gdns BT15	8	L8
Salisbury La BT7		
off Salisbury St	30	D5
Salisbury St BT7	30	C5
Samuel St BT1	20	M14
Sancroft St BT13	19	K13
Sandbrook Gdns BT4	21	T14
Sandbrook Gro BT4	21	T14
Sandbrook Pk BT4	21	T14
Sandford Av BT5	22	U16
Sandhill Dr BT5	22	U17
Sandhill Gdns BT5	22	V17
Sandhill Grn BT5		
off Sandhill Pk	22	V17
Sandhill Par BT5	22	V17
Sandhill Pk BT5	22	U17
Sandhurst Ct BT9		
off Colenso Par	26	M19
Sandhurst Dr BT9	26	M20
Sandhurst Gdns BT9	26	M20
Sandhurst Rd BT7	20	N18
Sandown Dr BT5	22	V16
Sandown Pk BT5	22	W17
Sandown Pk S BT5	22	V17
Sandown Rd BT5	22	V17
Sandringham Ms BT5	22	X16
Sandringham St BT9	26	K19
Sandymount St BT9	26	M20
Sandy Row BT12	30	B5
Sans Souci La BT9	26	L20
Sans Souci Pk BT9	26	L20
Santiago St BT13		
off Madras St	19	J13
Sarajac Cres BT14	8	J8
Sark St BT4	21	R15
Saul St BT5		
off Vulcan St	21	Q15
Saunders Cl BT4	21	R15
Saunderson Ct BT14		
off Glenpark St	13	J12
Sawel Hill BT11	24	D21
Schomberg Av BT4	22	X14
Schomberg Dr BT12	30	B6
Schomberg Lo BT4	22	X14
Schomberg Pk BT4	22	X14
Schomberg St BT12	30	B6
School Ct BT4	17	X11
School Rd BT8	27	Q24
Scotch Row BT4		
off Newtownards Rd	21	R15
Scotts Ct BT4	21	T16
Scotts Ms BT4	21	T16
Scrabo St BT5	31	G1
Seabank Par BT15	14	N9
Seabourne Par BT15	14	M9
Seaforde Ct BT5		
off Seaforde St	21	Q15
Seaforde Gdns BT5		
off Seaforde St	21	Q15
Seaforde St BT5	21	Q15
Seagrove Par BT15	14	N9
Seagrove Pl BT15		
off Premier Dr	14	M9
Seaholm Par BT15	14	N9
Sealands Par BT15	14	N9
Seal Rd BT3	15	R9
Seamount BT15	14	N9
Seamount Par BT15	14	N9
Seapark Av, Hol. BT18	11	AA5
Seapark Cl, Hol. BT18	11	AA5
Seapark Dr BT15	14	N9
Seapark Gro, Hol. BT18	11	BB5
Seapark Ms, Hol. BT18	11	AA5
Seapark Rd, Hol. BT18	11	AA4
Seapark Ter, Hol. BT18	11	AA5
Seascape Par BT15	14	M9
Seaview Cl BT15	14	N11
Seaview Dr BT15	14	M9
Seaview Gdns BT15	14	N9
Seaview St BT15	14	N11
Seaview Ter, Hol. BT18		
off Birch Dr	11	AA6
Sefton Dr BT4	22	U15
Sefton Pk BT4	22	U15
Selby Ct BT12	19	K16
Selby Wk BT12		
off Selby Ct	19	K16
Selkirk Row BT5		
off Granton Pk	23	AA17
Serpentine Gdns, New.		
BT36	9	M4
Serpentine Par, New.		
BT36	9	N4
Serpentine Rd, New.		
BT36	9	M4
Servia St BT12	19	K16
Sevastopol St BT13	19	J15
Severn St BT4	21	S15
Seymour La BT1		
off Seymour St	31	E3
Seymour Row BT1	31	E3
Seymour St BT1	31	E3
Seymour St BT2	31	E3
Shaftesbury Av BT7	20	N18
Shaftesbury Sq BT2	30	C6
Shalom Pk BT6	28	V21
Shamrock Ct BT6		
off Mount St S	21	Q17
Shamrock Pl BT6	21	Q17
Shamrock St BT6		
off Shamrock St	21	Q17
Shamrock St BT6	21	Q17
Shancoole Pk BT14	8	J7
Shandarragh Pk BT15	8	K8
Shandon Ct BT5	28	W20
Shandon Hts BT5		
off Lower Braniel Rd	29	X20
Shandon Pk BT5	22	W18
Shaneen Pk BT14	8	J7
Shangarry Pk BT14	8	K7
Shankill Par BT13	20	L14
Shankill Rd BT13	19	J14
Shankill Ter BT13		
off North		
Boundary St	20	L14
Shanlieve Pk BT14	8	K7
Shanlieve Rd BT11	24	E20
Shannon Ct BT14	19	K13
Shannon St BT14	19	K13
Shanvis Ct BT13	19	K15
Sharman Cl BT9	26	M22
Sharman Dr BT9	26	M22
Sharman Gdns BT9	26	M22
Sharman Pk BT9	26	M22
Sharman Rd BT9	26	M21
Sharman Way BT9	26	M22
Shaws Av BT11	24	C21
Shaws Cl BT11	24	B20
Shaws Ct BT11	24	C21
Shaws Pk BT11	24	C21
Shaws Pl BT11	24	C21
Shaws Rd BT11	24	B20
Shaw St BT4	22	U15
Shelbourne Rd BT6	27	R19
Sherbrook Cl BT13	20	L14
Sherbrook Ter BT13		
off Denmark St	20	L14
Sheridan Ct BT15		
off Sheridan St	20	M13
Sheridan St BT15	20	M13
Sheriff St BT5		
off Vulcan St	21	Q15
Sheringhurst Ct BT15	9	N7
Sheringhurst Pk BT15	9	N7
Sherwood St BT6	21	Q17
Sheskin Way BT6	27	R21
Shiels St BT12	19	H17
Shimna Cl BT6	27	R20
Shipbuoy St BT15	20	N13
Shore Cres BT15	9	N6
Shore Rd BT15	14	N10
Shore Rd, Hol. BT18	11	Z5
Short Strand BT5	21	Q15
Short St BT1	20	P13
Shrewsbury Dr BT9	25	H23
Shrewsbury Gdns BT9	25	H23
Shrewsbury Pk BT9	25	J23
Sicily Pk BT10	25	F23
Silver Birch Cts BT13	19	K14
Silvergrove, The BT6	27	S20
Silverstream Av BT14	13	G9
Silverstream Cres BT14	13	G9
Silverstream Dr BT14	13	G9
Silverstream Gdns		
BT14	13	G9
Silverstream Par BT14	13	G9
Silverstream Pk BT14	13	G9
Silverstream Rd BT14	13	G9
Silverstream Ter BT14	13	G9
Silvio St BT13	19	K13
Sinclair Rd BT3	15	Q11
Sinclair St BT5	22	V16
Sintonville Av BT5	21	T16
Siulnamona Ct BT11		
off Aitnamona Cres	24	D19
Skegoneill Av BT15	14	L9
Skegoneill Dr BT15	14	M10
Skegoneill St BT15	14	N10
Skipper St BT1	31	E1
Skipton St BT5	21	S16
Slemish Way BT11	24	E20
Sliabh Dubh Glen BT12	18	F16
Sliabh Dubh La BT12	19	G16
Sliabh Dubh Path BT12	19	G16
Sliabh Dubh Vw BT12	18	F16
Sliabh Dubh Wk BT12	19	G16
Slieveban Dr BT11	24	D21
Slievecoole Pk BT14	8	K7
Slievedarragh Pk BT14	8	J7
Slievegallion Dr BT11	24	D20
Slievegoland Pk, New.		
BT36	9	M4
Slievemoyne Pk BT15	8	L8
Slievetoye Pk BT14	8	J7
Sloan Ct BT9	25	J19
Smithfield Mkt BT1		
off Smithfield Sq N	30	C1
Smithfield Sq N BT1	30	C1
Snugville St BT13	19	K14
Solway St BT4	21	R15
Somerdale Gdns BT13	13	G11
Somerdale Pk BT14	13	G12
Somerset St BT7	27	P20
Somerton Cl BT15	8	L8
Somerton Ct BT15	14	M9
Somerton Dr BT15	14	M9
Somerton Gdns BT15	14	M9
Somerton Gra BT15	9	M7
Somerton Ms BT15	14	M9
Somerton Pk BT15	9	M8
Somerton Rd BT15	9	M8
Somme Dr BT6	27	S21
Sorella St BT12	19	J16
Soudan St BT12	19	J18
South Bk BT6	27	R21
South Cl, Hol. BT18	11	Z8
South Grn BT11	24	D20
Southland Dale BT5	28	W20
South Link BT11	24	E20
South Par BT7	27	P20
Southport Ct BT14		
off Mountview St	14	K12
South Sperrin BT5	23	AA17
Southview Cotts BT7		
off Stranmillis Embk	26	N19
Southview St BT7	26	N19
Southwell St BT15	20	N13
Spamount St BT15	14	M12
Spencer St, Hol. BT18	11	AA6
Sperrin Dr BT5	23	AA17
Sperrin Pk BT5	23	AA17
Spiers Pl BT13	19	K14
Spinnershill La BT14		
off Old Mill Rd	12	E9
Spinner Sq BT12		
off Leeson St	19	J16
Spires, The, Hol. BT18	11	BB7
Spires Mall Shop BT1	30	C3
Springdale Gdns BT13	19	G15
Springfield Av BT12	19	H15
Springfield Cl BT13	18	F15
Springfield Ct BT12	19	H15
Springfield Cres BT12	19	H15
Springfield Dr BT12	19	H15
Springfield Hts BT13	18	E15
Springfield Meadows		
BT13	19	G15
Springfield Par BT13	19	G15
Springfield Pk BT13	18	F15
Springfield Rd BT12	18	D17
Springhill Av BT12	18	F16
Springhill Cl BT12	18	F16
Springhill Cres BT12	18	F16
Springhill Dr BT12	18	F16
Springhill Gdns BT12	18	F16
Springhill Gro BT12	18	F16
Springhill Hts BT12	18	F16
Springhill Ri BT12	18	F16
Springmadden Ct BT12		
off Springhill Cres	18	F16
Springmartin Rd BT13	18	F15
Springmeadow BT12	19	J16
Spring Pl BT16		
off Spring St	21	Q16
Spring St BT6	21	Q17
Springvale Dr BT14	13	F9
Springvale Gdns BT14	13	F10
Springvale Par BT14	13	F9
Springvale Pk BT14	13	F9
Springview Wk BT13		
off Malcolmson St	19	J16
Squires Hill Cres BT14	13	F9
Squires Hill Pk BT14	13	F9
Squires Hill Rd BT14	13	F8
Squires Vw BT14	13	F9
Stables, The BT4	22	X13
Stanfield Pl BT7	31	F4
Stanfield Row BT7		
off Lower Stanfield St	31	G4
Stanhope Dr BT13	20	L14
Stanhope St BT13	20	L14
Stanley Ct BT12	30	A3
Stanley La BT15		
off Little York St	20	N14
Stanley Pl BT15		
off Little York St	20	N14
Stanley St BT12	30	A3
Station Ms (Sydenham)		
BT4	22	V13
Station Rd BT4	22	U13
Station St BT3	31	G1
Station St Flyover BT3	31	G1
Steam Mill La BT1	20	N14
Steens Back Row BT5		
off Abetta Par	21	T17
Stephen St BT1	20	N14
Stewarts Pl, Hol. BT18		
off Strand Av	11	AA5
Stewartstown Av BT11	24	B21
Stewartstown Gdns		
BT11	24	B21
Stewartstown Ms BT11		
off Stewartstown Av	24	C22
Stewartstown Pk BT11	24	B21
Stewartstown Rd BT11	24	B22
Stewart St BT7	31	G5
Stirling Av BT6	28	T20
Stirling Gdns BT6	27	S20
Stirling Rd BT6	27	S20
Stockmans Av BT11	25	F21
Stockmans Ct BT11	25	F21
Stockmans Cres BT11	25	F21
Stockmans Dr BT11		
off Stockmans Av	25	F20
Stockmans Gdns BT11		
off Stockmans Av	25	F21
Stockmans La BT9	25	F21
Stockmans La BT11	25	F21
Stockmans Pk BT11	25	F21
Stockmans Way BT9	24	E22
Stoneycairn Ct BT14		
off Mountainhill Rd	12	E9
Stoney Rd BT6	23	BB15
Stoney Rd (Dundonald)		
BT16	23	BB15
Stonyford St BT5	31	S16
Stormont Castle BT4	23	AA14
Stormont Ct BT4	23	Z16
Stormont Ms BT5	23	Z16
Stormont Pk BT4	23	Y16

45

Name	Map	Grid
Stormont Rd BT3	15	Q11
Stormont Vil BT4	23	Z14
Stormont Wd BT4	23	Z16
Stormount Cres BT5		
off Stormount St	21	R16
Stormount La BT5	21	R16
Stormount St BT5	21	R16
Stornoway Row BT5		
off Granton Pk	23	AA17
Stracam Cor BT6	27	R21
Straight, The BT6	27	R21
Strand Av, Hol. BT18	11	Z5
Strandburn Ct BT4		
off Strandburn Gdns	21	T14
Strandburn Cres BT4	22	U14
Strandburn Dr BT4	22	U14
Strandburn Gdns BT4	21	T14
Strandburn Par BT4	21	T14
Strandburn Pk BT4	22	U14
Strandburn St BT4	21	T14
Strand Cl BT5		
off Vulcan St	21	Q15
Strand Ct BT5		
off Avoniel Rd	21	S16
Strand Ms BT5	21	Q15
Strand Ms, Hol. BT18	11	Z5
Strand Studios BT4		
off Holywood Rd	22	U15
Strandview St BT9	26	M20
Strand Wk BT5		
off Vulcan St	21	Q15
Strangford Av BT9	25	H23
Stranmillis Embk BT7	26	M20
Stranmillis Embk BT9	26	N19
Stranmillis Gdns BT9	26	M20
Stranmillis Ms BT9	26	M20
Stranmillis Pk BT9	26	M20
Stranmillis Reach BT7		
off Stranmillis Embk	26	N19
Stranmillis Rd BT9	26	K22
Stranmillis St BT9	26	M20
Stratford Gdns BT14	13	H11
Strathearn Ct, Hol. BT18	11	Y7
Strathearn Ms BT4	22	V15
Strathearn Pk BT4	22	X13
Stratheden St BT15	14	M12
Strathmore Pk BT15	8	L7
Strathmore Pk N BT15	8	L7
Strathmore Pk S BT15	8	L7
Strathroy Pk BT14	13	H11
Stroud St BT12	30	B6
Sturgeon St BT12		
off Linfield Rd	30	B6
Suffolk Av BT11	24	B22
Suffolk Cres BT11	24	C22
Suffolk Dr BT11	24	B22
Suffolk Par BT11	24	B22
Sugarfield St BT13	19	J14
Sullivan Cl, Hol. BT18	11	Z6
Sullivan Pl, Hol. BT18	11	Z6
Sullivan St, Hol. BT18	11	AA5
Sultan Sq BT12		
off Servia St	19	K16
Sultan Way BT12		
off Osman St	19	K16
Summerhill Av BT5	23	Z17
Summerhill Ct BT4	14	K12
Summerhill Dr BT5		
off Summerhill Pk	23	Z16
Summerhill Par BT5	23	Z16
Summerhill Pk BT5	23	Z16
Summer St BT14	14	K12
Sunbury Av BT5	22	U16
Sunderland Rd BT6	27	S20
Sunningdale Dr BT14	8	J8
Sunningdale Gdns BT14	8	H8
Sunningdale Grn BT14	8	H8
Sunningdale Gro BT14	8	J8
Sunningdale Pk BT14	8	J8
Sunningdale Pk N BT14	8	J8
Sunninghill Dr BT14	13	J9
Sunninghill Gdns BT14	8	J8
Sunninghill Pk BT14	8	J8
Sunnyside Cres BT7	26	N20
Sunnyside Dr BT7	26	N20
Sunnyside Pk BT7	26	N21
Sunnyside St BT7	26	N20
Sunwich St BT4	21	Q18
Surrey St BT9	25	J20
Susan St BT5	21	R15
Sussex Pl BT2	31	E4
Swift Pl BT6		
off Swift St	21	Q16
Swift St BT6	21	Q16
Sycamore Gro BT4	22	U15
Sydenham Av BT4	22	V15
Sydenham Bypass BT3	21	S14
Sydenham Cres BT4	22	U14
Sydenham Dr BT4	22	U15
Sydenham Gdns BT4	22	U14
Sydenham Pk BT4	22	U14
Sydenham Rd BT3	20	P14
Sydney St W BT13	19	J13
Sylvan St BT14	14	K12
Symons St BT12	19	K17
Synnga St BT15		
off Upper Mervue St	14	M12

T

Name	Map	Grid
Talbot St BT1	20	M14
Tamar Ct BT4		
off Tamar St	21	S15
Tamar St BT4	21	S15
Tamery Pass BT6	21	R17
Tamery St BT6	21	R17
Tarawood, Hol. BT18	11	BB4
Tarawood Ms BT8	26	N23
Tardree Pk BT11	24	E20
Tasmania St BT13	19	K13
Tates Av BT9	26	K19
Tates Av BT12	19	J18
Tates Ms BT9	26	K19
Taunton Av BT15	9	M7
Tavanagh St BT12	19	J18
Taylor St BT12		
off Wellwood St	30	C5
Tedburn Pk BT14	13	G10
Telfair St BT1	31	E2
Templemore Av BT5	21	R15
Templemore Cl BT5		
off Templemore St	21	R16
Templemore Pl BT5		
off Beersbridge Rd	21	S17
Templemore St BT5	21	R16
Temple St BT5	21	S16
Tennent St BT13	19	J14
Tern St BT4	21	R15
Teutonic Gdns BT12	30	B6
Thalia St BT12	19	K18
Thames St BT12	19	H17
Thames St BT12	19	J17
Theodore St BT12		
off Grosvenor Rd	19	K16
Thiepval Av BT6	27	S20
Third St BT13	19	K15
Thirlmere Gdns BT15	8	K8
Thistle Ct BT5	21	R16
Thomas St BT15	20	M14
Thompson St BT5	21	Q16
Thompson Wf Rd BT3	15	R12
Thorburn Pk, New. BT36	9	M4
Thorburn Rd, New. BT36	9	M4
Thornberry Av BT14	12	D9
Thornberry Cl BT14	12	D9
Thornberry Hill BT14	12	D9
Thornberry Ms BT14	12	D9
Thornberry Rd BT14	12	D9
Thorndale Av BT14	14	L12
Thorndyke St BT5	21	R16
Thornhill Cres BT5	23	Y16
Thornhill Dr BT5	23	Y16
Thornhill Gdns BT9		
off Marlborough Pk S	26	K21
Thornhill Gro BT5	23	Y17
Thornhill Malone BT9	26	K21
Thornhill Ms BT5	23	Y17
Thornhill Par BT5	23	Y17
Thornhill Pk BT5	23	Y16
Tierney Gdns BT12	30	B6
Tildarg Av BT11	24	B23
Tildarg St BT6	21	R18
Tillysburn Dr BT4		
off Tillysburn Pk	16	W12
Tillysburn Gro BT4	16	W12
Tillysburn Pk BT4	16	W12
Timbey Pk BT7	26	N20
Titania St BT6	21	R18
Tivoli Gdns BT15	8	K8
Tobergill St BT13	19	J14
Tokio Gdns BT15	8	L8
Tollnamona Ct BT11		
off Aitnamona Cres	24	D19
Tomb St BT1	20	N14
Toronto St BT6	21	Q17
Torrens Av BT14	13	J11
Torrens Ct BT14		
off Torrens Rd	14	K11
Torrens Cres BT14	13	J11
Torrens Dr BT14	13	J11
Torrens Gdns BT14	13	J11
Torrens Par BT14	13	J11
Torrens Rd BT14	14	K11
Torr Way BT10	25	F24
Tower Ct BT5		
off Susan St	21	R15
Tower St BT5	21	R15
Townhall St BT1	31	F2
Townsend St BT13	30	B1
Townsley St BT4		
off Newtownards Rd	21	S15
Trafalgar St BT15	20	N13
Trainfield St BT15	14	M12
Trassey Cl BT6	27	R20
Trenchard BT11	24	B23
Trench Av BT11	24	D22
Trench Pk BT11	24	D22
Trevor St, Hol. BT18	11	Z6
Trigo Par BT6	28	T19
Trillick Ct BT5		
off Trillick St	21	R17
Trillick St BT5	21	R16
Trinity St BT13	20	M14
Trostan Gdns BT11	24	E21
Trostan Way BT11	24	E20
Tudor Av BT6	28	T21
Tudor Dale BT4	22	V13
Tudor Dr BT6	28	T21
Tudor Gro BT13	19	K13
Tudor Oaks, Hol. BT18	11	AA5
Tudor Pl BT13	19	K13
Tullagh Pk BT11	24	C20
Tullyard Way BT6	28	U20
Tullymore Dr BT11	24	C20
Tullymore Gdns BT11	24	C20
Tullymore Wk BT11	24	C21
Turin St BT12	19	K16
Twaddell Av BT13	19	G13
Tweskard Lo BT4	23	Y13
Tweskard Pk BT4	23	Y14
Twiselside, Hol. BT18	11	AA6
Tyndale Cres BT14	8	H8
Tyndale Dr BT14	8	H8
Tyndale Gdns BT14	8	H8
Tyndale Grn BT14	8	H8
Tyndale Gro BT14	13	G8
Tyne St BT13	19	K14
Tyrone St BT13	20	M14

U

Name	Map	Grid
Ulsterdale St BT5	21	T16
Ulster St BT1	31	E1
Ulsterville Av BT9	19	K18
Ulsterville Dr BT9	19	K18
Ulsterville Gdns BT9	19	K18
Ulsterville Pl BT9		
off Belgravia Av	20	L18
Uniondale St BT5	21	T16
Union St BT1	20	M14
Unity Wk BT13		
off Plunkett St	20	M14
University Av BT7	20	M18
University Rd BT7	26	L19
University Sq BT7	20	M18
University Sq Ms BT7	20	M18
University St BT7	20	M18
University Ter BT7		
off University Rd	26	L19
Upper Arthur St BT1	31	E3
Upper Braniel Rd BT5	28	W22
Upper Canning St BT15	14	M12
Upper Castle Pk BT15	8	K7
Upper Cavehill La BT14	8	H6
Upper Cavehill Rd BT15	8	K7
Upper Charleville St BT13	19	K13
Upper Ch La BT1		
off Ann St	31	E2
Upper Clara Cres BT5		
off Clara Av	21	T17
Upper Ctyd BT7	26	N21
Upper Cres BT7	20	M18
Upper Cres La BT7		
off Mount Charles	20	M18
Upper Frank St BT5	21	R17
Upper Galwally BT8	27	Q23
Upper Glenfarne St BT13	19	K13
Upper Hightown Rd BT14	13	G7
Upper Knockbreda Rd BT6	27	Q23
Upper Knockbreda Rd BT8	27	Q23
Upperlands Wk BT5		
off Abbey Pk	23	AA17
Upper Meadow St BT15	14	M12
Upper Meenan St BT13	19	K14
Upper Mervue St BT15	14	M12
Upper Newtownards Rd BT4	21	T16
Upper Newtownards Rd (Dundonald) BT16	23	BB16
Upper Queen St BT1	30	C3
Upper Riga St BT13	19	J14
Upper Springfield Rd BT12	24	B19
Upper Springfield Rd (Hannahstown) BT17	24	B19
Upper Stanfield St BT7		
off Lower Stanfield St	31	G4
Upper Townsend Ter BT13	20	L14
Upton Av BT10	24	D24
Upton Cotts BT11	18	E18
Upton Ct BT11	18	E18
Upton Pk BT10	24	E24
Utility St BT12	30	A6
Utility Wk BT12	19	K17

V

Name	Map	Grid
Valleyside Cl BT12	19	H15
Vancouver Dr BT15	14	L10
Vandyck Cres, New. BT36	9	M4
Vandyck Dr, New. BT36	9	M4
Vandyck Gdns, New. BT36	9	N4
Vara Dr BT13	19	H14
Vauxhall Pk BT9	26	M22
Velsheda Ct BT14	13	H11
Velsheda Pk BT14	13	H11
Velsheda Way BT14	13	H11
Ventry La BT2	30	C5
Ventry St BT2	30	C5
Vere Foster Wk BT12		
off Moyard Cres	18	E15
Verner St BT7	31	F3
Vernon Ct BT7	30	D6
Vernon St BT7	20	M18
Veryan Gdns, New. BT36	9	N4
Vicarage St BT5	21	R16
Vicinage Pk BT14	20	L13
Vicinage Pl BT14		
off Vicinage Pk	20	L13
Victoria Av BT4	22	U13
Victoria Ct BT4	22	V14
Victoria Dr BT4	22	U13
Victoria Gdns BT15	8	K8
Victoria Par BT15	20	M13
Victoria Rd BT3	21	Q13
Victoria Rd BT4	22	U13
Victoria Rd, Hol. BT18	11	AA5
Victoria Sq BT1	31	E2
Victoria St BT1	31	E1

Name	No	Grid
Victor Pl BT6	21	Q16
Vidor Ct BT4		
off Victoria Dr	22	U14
Vidor Gdns BT4	22	U14
Village Grn, The BT6	27	S19
Violet St BT12	19	J16
Vionville Cl BT5	23	BB18
Vionville Ct BT5		
off Vionville Ri	23	BB18
Vionville Grn BT5		
off Vionville Ri	23	BB18
Vionville Hts BT5		
off Vionville Ri	23	BB18
Vionville Pk BT5		
off Vionville Ri	23	BB18
Vionville Pl BT5	23	BB18
Vionville Ri BT5	23	BB18
Vionville Vw BT5	23	BB18
Vionville Way BT5		
off Vionville Ri	23	BB18
Virginia St BT7		
off Elm St	30	D6
Virginia Way BT7	30	D6
Vistula St BT13	19	J13
Voltaire Gdns, New. BT36	9	N4
Vulcan Ct BT5		
off Vulcan St	21	Q15
Vulcan Gdns BT5		
off Seaforde St	21	Q15
Vulcan Link BT5		
off Vulcan St	21	Q15
Vulcan St BT5	21	Q15

W

Name	No	Grid
Walbeck St BT15		
off Dawson St	20	M13
Walker Ct BT6	21	R17
Walkers La BT1		
off Frederick St	20	M14
Wallasey Pk BT14	13	H9
Walled Gdn, The BT4	22	X13
Wall St BT13	20	M14
Walmer St BT7	26	N20
Walnut Ct BT7	31	E6
Walnut Ms BT7	31	E6
Walnut St BT7	31	E6
Wandsworth Ct BT4	22	W16
Wandsworth Cres BT4	22	W16
Wandsworth Dr BT4	22	W15
Wandsworth Gdns BT4	22	W15
Wandsworth Par BT4	22	W16
Wandsworth Pl BT4		
off Campbell Pk Av	22	W15
Wandsworth Rd BT4	22	W15
Wansbeck St BT9	26	M21
Ward St BT12	19	K15
Waring St BT1	31	E1
Warren Gro BT5	29	X20
Waterford Gdns BT13	19	J15
Waterford St BT13	19	J16
Waterford Way BT13		
off Waterford St	19	J16
Waterloo Gdns BT15	9	M6
Waterloo Pk BT15	8	L6
Waterloo Pk N BT15	8	L6
Waterloo Pk S BT15	8	L6
Watermouth Cres BT12	19	G15
Waterville St BT13	19	J15
Watkins Rd BT3	15	P12
Watt St BT6	21	Q18
Wauchope Ct BT12		
off Connaught St	19	K17
Waveney Av BT15	9	N7
Waveney Dr BT15	9	N7
Waveney Gro BT15	9	N7
Waveney Hts BT15	9	N7
Waveney Pk BT15	9	N7
Wayland St BT5	21	S17
Wayside Cl BT5	28	W20
Weavers Ct BT12	30	A5
Weavershill Ct BT14	12	E9
Weavershill La BT14	13	F9
Weavershill Ms BT14	12	E9
Weavershill Rd BT14	12	E9
Weavershill Wk BT14		
off Mountainhill Rd	13	F9
Welland St BT4	21	S15
Wellesley Av BT9	26	L19
Wellington Ct BT1		
off Wellington St	30	C3
Wellington La BT9	26	L19
Wellington Pk BT9	26	L19
Wellington Pk Av BT9	26	L19
Wellington Pk Ter BT9	26	L19
Wellington Pl BT1	30	C3
Wellington St BT1	30	C3
Well Pl BT6	21	Q17
Wellwood Av BT4	21	T14
Wellwood Cl BT4		
off Wellwood Av	21	T14
Wellwood St BT12	30	B5
Welsh St BT7	31	F4
Wesley Ct BT12		
off Donegall Rd	30	C6
Wesley St BT12		
off Stroud St	30	C6
West Bk Cl BT3	15	S8
West Bk Dr BT3	15	S8
West Bk Link BT3	15	S8
West Bk Rd BT3	15	S8
West Bk Way BT3	15	S8
Westbourne St BT5	21	R15
West Circular Cres BT13	19	G14
West Circular Rd BT13	19	G15
Westcott St BT5		
off Bloomfield Av	21	T16
West Grn, Hol. BT18	11	Z7
Westhill Way BT12		
off Glenalina Cres	18	E17
Westland Cotts BT14	14	K9
Westland Dr BT14	14	K10
Westland Gdns BT14	14	K10
Westland Rd BT14	13	J10
Westland Way BT14	14	K10
Westlink BT12	20	L14
Westlink BT13	20	L14
West Link, Hol. BT18	11	Z7
Westminster Av BT4	21	T15
Westminster Av N BT4		
off Westminster Av	21	T15
Westminster St BT7	20	N18
Weston Dr BT9	25	G22
Westrock Ct BT12	18	F16
Westrock Cres BT12	19	G16
Westrock Dr BT12	18	F16
Westrock Gdns BT12	18	F16
Westrock Grn BT12	18	F17
Westrock Gro BT12		
off Westrock Gdns	19	G16
Westrock Ms BT12	19	G16
Westrock Par BT12	18	F17
Westrock Pk BT12		
off Westrock Gdns	18	F16
Westrock Pl BT12	19	G17
Westrock Sq BT12	19	G16
Westrock Way BT12	19	G16
Westview Pas BT12		
off Glenalina Cres	18	E17
Westway Cres BT13	18	E13
Westway Dr BT13	18	F13
Westway Gdns BT13	12	E12
Westway Gro BT13	18	F13
Westway Hill BT13	18	E13
Westway Par BT13	18	F13
Westway Pk BT13	18	F13
Wheatfield Ct BT14	13	G10
Wheatfield Cres BT14	13	G11
Wheatfield Dr BT14	13	G10
Wheatfield Gdns BT14	13	G11
Whincroft Rd BT5	28	W19
Whincroft Way BT5	28	W20
Whitecliff Cres BT12	18	F17
Whitecliff Dr BT12		
off Whiterock Rd	18	F17
Whitecliff Par BT12	18	F17
Whiterock Cl BT12		
off Whiterock Rd	18	E17
Whiterock Cres BT12	18	F17
Whiterock Gdns BT12	18	F17
Whiterock Gro BT12	18	E17
Whiterock Par BT12	18	F17
Whiterock Rd BT12	18	D15
Whitewell Ct, New. BT36	9	N4
Whitewell Cres, New. BT36	9	N4
Whitewell Dr, New. BT36	9	N4
Whitewell Par, New. BT36	9	N4
Whitla St BT15	15	P12
Wigton St BT13		
off Percy Pl	20	L14
Wildflower Way BT12	25	H20
Wilgar Cl BT4		
off Dundela St	22	U15
Wilgar St BT4	22	U15
Willesden Pk BT9	26	M22
William Alexander Pk BT10	24	D24
William St BT1	20	M14
William St S BT1	31	E2
Willowbank Cres BT6	27	S22
Willowbank Dr BT6	27	R22
Willowbank Gdns BT15	14	L10
Willowbank Pk BT6	27	R22
Willowfield Av BT6		
off Willowfield Par	21	R17
Willowfield Cres BT6	21	R17
Willowfield Dr BT6	21	R17
Willowfield Gdns BT6	21	R17
Willowfield Par BT6	21	R17
Willowfield St BT6	21	R17
Willowfield Wk BT6	21	R17
Willowholme Cres BT6		
off Willowholme Par	21	R18
Willowholme Dr BT6	21	R18
Willowholme Par BT6	21	R18
Willowholme St BT6	21	R18
Willows, The BT6	27	S22
Willow St BT12	30	A3
Willowvale Av BT11	24	C22
Willowvale Gdns BT11	24	C22
Willowvale Ms BT11		
off Willowvale Gdns	24	C22
Wilshere Dr BT4	22	W13
Wilsons Ct BT1		
off Ann St	31	E2
Wilson St BT13	30	B1
Wilton Ct Ms BT13		
off Canmore St	19	J14
Wilton Gdns BT13	19	J14
Wilton St BT13	19	J15
Winchester Ct BT13		
off Ambleside St	19	J13
Windermere Gdns BT15	8	K8
Windsor Av BT9	26	K19
Windsor Av, Hol. BT18	11	AA6
Windsor Av N BT9	26	L20
Windsor Cl BT9	26	K20
Windsor Ct BT9		
off Windsor Pk	26	K20
Windsor Dr BT9	25	J19
Windsor Manor BT9	26	K19
Windsor Ms BT9	26	K20
Windsor Pk BT9	26	K20
Windsor Rd BT9	25	J19
Winecellar Entry BT1		
off Rosemary St	30	D1
Winetavern St BT1	30	C1
Wingrove Gdns BT5	21	T17
Winston Gdns BT5	22	W16
Witham St BT4	21	S15
Wofend Dr BT14	13	F9
Wofend Way BT14		
off Hazelbrook Dr	13	F8
Wolff Cl BT4	21	Q15
Wolff Rd BT3	15	S11
Wolfhill Av BT14		
off Ligoniel Pl	12	E9
Wolfhill Av S BT14	12	D9
Wolfhill Dr BT14	12	D9
Wolfhill Gdns BT14	12	D8
Wolfhill Gro BT14	12	D8
Wolfhill Manor BT14	12	D8
Wolfhill Rd BT13	12	D10
Wolfhill Rd BT14	12	C8
Wolfhill Vw BT14		
off Mill Av	12	E8
Wolseley St BT7	20	M18
Woodbine Ct BT11	24	B22
Woodbourne Cres BT11	24	B22
Woodburn Dr BT15	8	K8
Woodburn St BT13		
off Downing St	19	K14
Woodcot Av BT5	21	T17
Woodcroft Hts BT5	28	W20
Woodcroft Ri BT5	28	W20
Wood End, Hol. BT18	11	Z8
Woodland Av BT14	14	L11
Woodland Gra BT11	24	D23
Woodlands, Hol. BT18	11	BB6
Woodlands Ct BT4	22	X15
Woodlee Ct BT5	21	S17
Woodstock Link BT6	21	Q16
Woodstock Pl BT6	21	Q16
Woodstock Rd BT6	21	Q16
Woodvale Av BT13	19	H14
Woodvale Dr BT13	13	H12
Woodvale Gdns BT13	13	H12
Woodvale Par BT13	19	H13
Woodvale Pass BT13	19	H14
Woodvale Rd BT13	13	H12
Woodvale St BT13	19	H13
Woodview Dr BT5	29	Y19
Woodview Pl BT5	29	Y19
Woodview Ter BT5		
off Woodview Dr	29	Y19
Workman Av BT13	19	H14
Workman Rd BT3	15	S11
Wye St BT4		
off Dee St	21	S15
Wynard Pk BT5	22	X18
Wynchurch Av BT6	27	R22
Wynchurch Cl BT6		
off Wynchurch Rd	27	R22
Wynchurch Gdns BT6	27	R22
Wynchurch Pk BT6	27	R21
Wynchurch Rd BT6	27	R21
Wynchurch Ter BT6	27	Q22
Wynchurch Wk BT6	27	R22
Wyndham Dr BT14	14	K11
Wyndham St BT14	14	K11
Wynfield Ct BT5	22	U16
Wynford St BT5		
off Moorgate St	21	T16

Y

Name	No	Grid
Yarrow Ct BT14		
off Yarrow St	19	K13
Yarrow St BT14	19	K13
Yew St BT13	19	H13
York Cres BT15	14	N9
York Dr BT15	14	N9
Yorkgate Shop Cen BT15	20	N13
York La BT1	20	M14
York Link BT15	19	J13
York Par BT15	14	N9
York Pk BT15	14	N9
York Rd BT15	14	N10
York St BT15	20	M14
Yukon St BT4	21	S15

Tourist and travel information

Tourist information

Belfast Welcome Centre,
47 Donegall Place,
Belfast BT1 5AD
www.discovernorthernireland.com

028 9024 6609
048 9024 6609

Belfast International Airport

028 9448 4677
048 9448 4677

George Best Belfast City Airport

028 9093 5372
048 9093 5372

Airport information

Belfast International Airport,
Aldergrove
Belfast BT9 4AB
www.belfastairport.com

028 9448 4848
048 9448 4848

George Best Belfast City Airport,
Sydenham Bypass,
Belfast BT3 9JH
www.belfastcityairport.com

028 9093 9093
048 9093 9093

Map reference 16 U11

Ferry information

ISLE OF MAN STEAM PACKET CO.
www.steam-packet.com
Belfast to Douglas (April-September)

0871 222 1333
00 44 871 222 1333

NORFOLK LINE
www.norfolkline-ferries.co.uk
Belfast to Birkenhead

0844 499 0007
01 819 2999

STENA LINE www.stenaline.ie
Belfast to Stranraer

08705 707070
01 204 7777

Note: If phoning from GB and Northern Ireland use bold telephone number, if phoning from Republic of Ireland use italic telephone number.